TARGETING SUCCESS

FROM A WOMAN'S POINT OF VIEW
MARGARET CHRISTIE

MANAGE PTY. LTD.

First published 1986 by
William Heinemann Australia
in association with
René Gordon Pty Ltd
Republished 1992 by Manage Pty Ltd

Copyright © Margaret Christie 1986

Commissioned and produced by René Gordon Pty Ltd
Cover design by Ken Cato Design Pty Ltd, Melbourne
Typeset by Trade Graphics Pty Ltd, Melbourne
Printed and bound in Australia by The Book Printer, Victoria

National Library of Australia
Cataloguing in Publication data:

Christie, Margaret, 1940–
 Targeting success.

 Bibliography.
 ISBN 0 949208 05 1.

 1. Women—Life skills guides. 2. Self-actualization
 (Psychology). 3. Success. I. Title.

158'.1

All rights reserved. No part of this publication may be
reproduced, stored in a retrieval system or transmitted, in any
form or by any means, electronic, mechanical, recording or
otherwise, without the written permission of the copyright
owners.

The author and publisher have sought permission to reproduce
all copyright material in this book. They would like to thank
those who have kindly granted permission and also acknowledge
the few who have not responded.

ISBN 0 949208 05 1

All enquiries:
Manage Pty Ltd

Contents

Introduction
Part I   Aiming for the outer circles
CHAPTER   1   You can direct your life   1
   2   Are you a risk-taker?   10
   3   Is that all there is to life?   27
   4   What is this thing success?   45
   5   Getting there: values and goals   55
   6   Afraid of being successful?   72
   7   A career on your own terms   84
   8   The new you: living with it   99

Part II   Moving further in
CHAPTER   9   How far do you want to grow?   117
   10   Strategies and skills for you and your household   135
   11   Achieving visibility   160
   12   Organising yourself   180
   13   Women's groups: the new style entrepreneurs   190
   14   Wiles and styles: management, leadership and power   204
   15   The older and wiser you: pampering yourself   222
   16   What is the next stage for you and your daughters?   233

References and further reading   239
Index   244

To Neville for his ongoing support
in my targeting success.

To Antony and Catherine who make it worthwhile.

INTRODUCTION

This book is about my belief that women can target and achieve more success in their lives, on their own terms.

Although I have experienced the lack of planning, the assumed roles, the frustrations and the doubts so familiar to many women, I have also discovered opportunities that have allowed me to combine success in several careers with a husband, a good marriage and a family. This book reflects my belief that you do not always have to make black or white decisions about settling for a career or a family, that success for you may be different from the traditional view of achievement and that with acquired skills and organisation you can juggle many roles in life and still enjoy them.

I have written this book partly from my own search for meaning and satisfaction in life as a woman and partly because I have found that career planning has changed other people's lives as well. It is also based on my reading, observations, reflections and experiences over the years and on the results of the group and individual career planning programs I have developed. Working with and watching other women grow in their understanding of themselves, their skills and their ambitions has been rewarding for me. Sharing in their experiences has made my own life richer.

There are many books which motivate people to pick themselves up and strive for the top but these so often present life from a man's vantage point. They assume the entrenched view that the only way to achieve success is through the traditional pyramid-shaped organisation with its burdens of stress, single-mindedness and one-dimensional living. Not surprisingly, as far as women are concerned, these books often range from frustrating to offensive, for they assume a freedom of choice which many of us feel we do not have. And when caught in our traditional roles of chief babysitters, cooks and keepers of stability we do find it difficult to get out and look at the world from a particular vantage point of our own.

The challenge is to find our own ways of targeting success through enlarging our abilities to take risks, by increasing our self-esteem, by growing as people and perceiving and grasping the opportunities so often there for the taking.

So this book is about developing our abilities and raising our expectations so that we can recognise many more of the openings when they are offered to us. Once we acknowledge that we can choose to take hold of our lives then we are in a better position to accept – or reject – those opportunities.

Looking back on my own life it appears divided into two stages: before and after I became depressed. In the first part, despite a lack of conscious control over my own destiny, I was able to take advantage of varied opportunities that came my way. Long before I was aware of a pattern emerging, I acquired some of the basic skills of survival.

At school, at university and then as an Australian Volunteer Abroad, I was able to extend my horizons and learn something not only about working with others, but about myself. After two years in India, helping to set up a new school in Bihar, I returned to Australia.

I settled down: married, bought a house, taught in private schools and, later, went into business with my husband. This led to periods of severe depression as I tried to juggle looking after our first child with being the supportive wife, home help and business partner. The combination of roles was not conducive to raising my self-esteem. Obviously I had to do something about it. The process of resurrecting myself is the foundation for much of what follows in this book.

It is this process that tends to follow a spiral pattern rather than a straight line. Perhaps this is one of the more obvious differences between the accepted male and female career patterns. The male pattern of achievement tends to follow goals set in early years. It assumes a directness in moving towards that achievement and often ignores emotional needs or personal development along the way. Women, on the other hand, who choose to look after families, tend to discover other career objectives later in life. When this happens they are able to achieve them using a multi-faceted approach based on their wider experiences. Women who choose the straight line goal-oriented path early in their lives often have to make either/or choices between seeking personal happiness in relationships or having a family or a successful career.

For me the advantage of the spiral approach has been that it has released my potential for both success and contentment. Now eight years later I feel far more aware of who I am and what I can become than I ever did in the first stage of my life.

In this second stage I have, among other things, adopted two children, learnt how to print fabric, started and finished a post-graduate diploma in marketing, been president of Women in Management, commenced a business of my own, run courses I created myself and explored many ideas.

As a strategic consultant I work with organisations to develop marketing and business plans. I have come to focus particularly on the training of staff and management in companies that are growing, and changing as a result. I also enjoy the challenge of serving on several government bodies and the boards of a number of private companies.

Over the last few years my life has taken on a real sense of direction. For the first time I can look back on the goals I have attained and take pleasure from that achievement while looking forward to the many opportunities yet ahead. The wonderful thing I have found is that once you chart a broad course for your life you become aware of many more opportunities than you ever supposed were there for the taking.

This is the course that may lead you to new and waiting horizons. Bon voyage!

PART I

AIMING FOR THE OUTER CIRCLES

1 YOU CAN DIRECT YOUR LIFE

A man may think and say: 'When I finish school I will...'
'When I become head of this department I will...'
'I want to be good at playing golf.'
'I want to retire when I'm 50.'

And the man is serious about this. What he is saying reflects how he thinks of himself and where he sees his life going. Implicit is the setting of goals and the working to reach them, a process which others will respect and assist him in achieving.

Traditionally, this has not been so for women. A woman may be encouraged to think merely about what she will do to make a living as a stop gap until she gets married or meets a person with whom to share her life. Any career goals she has are often tempered by the wants of others and the assumption that her wants will somehow be defined and directed by events rather than by herself. This can affect her in several ways. If she does marry or form a permanent relationship or find she has responsibility for looking after dependants she may miss out on <u>learning how to take control of her life</u>. This makes it difficult for self-development later when she is free of dependants or recognises the need to take the helm.

Alternatively a woman may not want to marry. Or she may be divorced or have no children. A husband may die leaving a woman still young and perhaps inadequately cared for financially. In these situations a woman often takes stock of where she wants to go only once she accepts she has to support herself for the rest of her life.

Being able to work out the most productive and satisfying way to earn a living and develop her interests will require her to learn how to direct her life. Too often this happens only after fate thrusts self-responsibility on to us. But for more and more women, the decision to take control, to target success, is being seen as a free choice. We need to learn to do it before we have to, and practise it as part of our being able to live richer lives.

For the woman who marries, often the details of what she will do as a married woman or as a mother are vague and undefined. She may have romantic notions of the dream home in which she will live and the number of children she will have. But often she is unprepared for the roles and personal demands life with a partner and family make on her.

So frequently the adjustment a woman makes to living with another person leads to her losing control of her own life. This can mean leading a day-to-day existence often far removed from the way she lived as a single independent person or would prefer to live in a relationship.

If she has children she may find that the dreams she had of how she would look after them and enjoy their company rapidly turn to ashes. Becoming a parent is one of the commonest shared human experiences. But it is also the one for which we are least prepared. If you have children, one way of starting to take hold of your life is to explore how to feel more successful as a parent in your basic role of managing a family.

Paid work for what?

In today's world a woman may feel she has to go outside her home for paid work rather than admit she enjoys spending her time managing the house and doing the essential work of raising children. If that is your situation this book will help you to recognise how important your values as a homemaker are to you. Then you can work out how to live your life while gaining satisfaction from managing your home. Or you might develop a non-paid career path following your community interests. Some of these ideas are explored in Chapter Seven.

If earning money is the only reason for looking outside the home for work this book may help you to seek ways of making your work situation more effective in your life as a whole. Maybe this means examining what you would prefer to do to earn money and then making it happen. Maybe it will lead to finding other ways of feeling successful – through taking up hobbies or changing your lifestyle to suit your current values.

Whatever your situation, this book will encourage you to take a firm grip on life and begin directing it to meet some of your own needs as well as those of the people around you.

What this book will do

I have worked from the assumption that you can always begin to enrich your life and seize the opportunities around you no matter how old you are. I have included a number of exercises which are designed to lay the basis from which you can begin (or continue) to direct your own life.

Rather than merely preach about what you can do, this book aims to lead you into exploring this for yourself. The exercises are not intended to be difficult. There are no <u>right</u> answers. Any answers you find for yourself are correct for you now.

The book is presented in two parts. The first covers the mental and emotional preparation necessary before you can target success. For many of you, this may be familiar well-worn ground, yet for others it is a necessary precursor to any bid for success. Part II moves from personal preparation to action and attainment of a way of life of your choosing.

What were your dreams?

Many women have dreams as girls of what they would achieve besides being girlfriends, wives, mothers or emotional supports to others. Often these dreams are too fragile and precious to reveal to anyone else for fear of ridicule or there is no-one sympathetic enough to listen to them and encourage you. Perhaps the dreams seemed simply impossible at the time. Or maybe you did not explore what might make them come true.

I remember wanting to be a journalist but was discouraged by career counsellors at school. I was assured it was a very difficult career to break into and that opportunities as trainee journalists were virtually non-existent in country towns. I did not explore it any further.

Ideas of being an archaeologist were also scorned, but the career counsellors fell back on much more obscure reasons about the difficulties of being 'a woman on site'. As an inexperienced 14-year-old I did not fully understand those reasons but felt there were mysteries being hinted at that I would only come to comprehend with the fullness of time.

Later, of course, I realised that women could be archaeologists and explorers if they wanted to. The mysteries my vocational counsellors hinted at indicated the same attitudes of prejudice and conservatism which I was to encounter and fight against in future work situations.

Some of my other dreams centred around having a flat of my own which I decorated to suit myself. Those certainly came true! What dreams did you have as a child?

EXERCISE
Exploring dreams

Knowing more about yourself is very empowering; it enables you to grasp new knowledge and possibilities. All the exercises in this book are based on this concept. You should get your own book and start writing and exploring things about yourself.

Your first exercise is very simple – to reach back into your past and resurrect your dreams, whatever they were. Write them down in whatever form is comfortable for you:
- phrases
- poems.
- sentences

> Or, if you prefer, you can draw pictures or diagrams of your dreams – what you as a child thought you might make of your life before other events occurred that have determined your path so far.
>
> Once you have written down your dreams tick the ones you have made come true. These might be decorating a home, raising your children, building a house, finishing a technical course, developing a career or particular talent, or having the chance to travel.
>
> When you have written down any dreams you can remember, consider whether the ones still unfulfilled mean anything to you now. Sifting and sorting your dreams might be the first step you take towards making your own choice about your future.

I have mentioned being a journalist or an archaeologist as two of my own dreams. Other women have realised they wanted to be doctors, artists, veterinary surgeons, sportswomen, lawyers, scientists, actresses, writers, travellers, teachers or owners of their own businesses.

Some of them like Annabelle have made those dreams come true later in life.

Annabelle led an active life for many years raising a family and supporting her husband in his political career. This entailed organising parties for guests and playing hostess, often to foreign visitors.

When she was 37, Annabelle began to consider what she would really like to do with her own life. She realised that she had never developed her talent as an artist. Eventually she discussed this with her husband and he agreed to support her efforts. Annabelle now works in a cottage in the country most of the time, developing her skills far away from the social whirl. She still plays hostess occasionally, but her main efforts are in realising her postponed dream of being an artist.

We can make our own choices about simple things

Often as girlfriends, partners, wives and mothers we lose the ability to work out just what we would like to do about ordinary things. Believing we have to please others and fit in with their wishes, we simply lose touch with choosing for ourselves. We forget we have things that <u>we</u> want to do. We forget that we have our own preferences. How long is it since you:

- watched what you like on television?
- went to a movie of your choice?
- listened to your kind of music?
- did what you wanted for your holidays?
- spent weekends for your own relaxation and enjoyment?
- developed your own hobbies?
- worked at your own career?

Getting in touch with ourselves – who we are, our feelings, our dreams, our weaknesses, our strengths and skills, and what we can work to change, and, above all, our aspirations – enables us to begin to recognise what we would like to do and to follow up our choices with action.

The purpose of this book is to encourage you to start thinking of what you might like to do with your own life now, or soon, or in a few years' time when the children are older or whenever you are ready to consider your own needs as a person.

I believe that <u>the more you can get in touch with your feelings and know about yourself as a person the more power you have to take control of your life and where you are going</u>.

Adjusting relationships

This also means you can develop relationships to suit everyone's needs as people, including your own. When you start taking this approach your relationships with family and friends may need adjusting. The other people in your life have become used to seeing you in a certain way. In the beginning they will find it disconcerting, if not difficult, living with the new you.

Some of the difficulties may arise from the fact that you have made them dependent on you. Your first task would be to work to make them become more independent so you can be freed to be yourself. This takes time and effort. But in the long term it can be very rewarding for everyone.

It is often said: 'If you want to change others change yourself first.' Certainly, others find a happy person easier to live with than a discontented one. And I believe that taking control of your life can eventually lead to your being a happier person far more so than if you merely let life buffet you at its will. We may not always be able to influence what happens to us but we certainly can decide how we will react to those events. This is what taking control of our lives is all about.

Women already know survival tactics

An astute business consultant once said that most housewives were better organised than many managers. Women have to decide what they will do each day in order to keep the house going, food on the table, the dishes and clothes washed, not to mention the ongoing responsibility of parenting their children. Most women are managers in that they manage their homes. They make sure supplies are there in one way or another. If they do not do it themselves they organise others (eg other members of the family, house help or delivery services) to make sure the tasks are done.

You exhibit organisational skills every time you cook a meal, pack a picnic, organise a dinner party and pack up to go on a holiday. Running tuckshops, fêtes, street stalls, committees, conferences and businesses are simply extensions of these basic organisational principles.

Women can apply these principles by extending the skills already acquired in the domestic arena to other areas of their lives. Too often we say, dismissively, we are 'just housewives' without realising the skills we have learnt in that process. We fail to recognise the richness of the 'on the job' training that managing to cater for a family, working out 'industrial' disputes (often about demarcation issues), meeting deadlines (whenever we get children to school or elsewhere on time) and keeping the premises in reasonable order (maintenance and cleaning responsibilities) has provided for us. Transfer those skills to different situations and we begin to raise our heads high as we realise our potential to organise most tasks no matter where they are located.

In businesses or in organisations, many managers find it difficult to choose from the many tasks confronting them. Often it is easier for them to rush from crisis to crisis than to decide which jobs most need their attention.

Women as a matter of course not only work out their daily priorities but also often write down lists of things which need to be done – shopping lists for supplies, and memory-jolters. These survival tactics
- of deciding what needs to be done and what can be left till later, and
- making check lists to remember what needs to be done

form the basis of most time-management courses which motivate people, especially people in organisations, to change the habits of their work-lives. The concepts of time-management combined with decisions on goals and objectives and priorities give people a unique ability to direct their lives.

Since many of us already survive by possessing the skills of time-management we are at least halfway there. Then we can begin to extend our interests, take up courses, find work, achieve dormant desires, pursue careers and begin to take advantage of the opportunities all around us.

EXERCISE
Making lists and changing what to do
For this exercise, think back and write down in your

own private book the kinds of lists you used in the last fortnight. For example, shopping lists, appointments, clothes for holidays, things you had to do.

Check whether you did all the things you listed. Then write down a new list of any unfinished business or actions or supplies unpurchased.

What did you do about anything which you could not finish? Are they still relevant? If not cross them off. Now decide when you will work on your new list.

To use your lists effectively you need to keep track of any unfinished actions and put them down as part of your next list.

Here are some ideas which may help you if you have not yet found a satisfactory way of keeping lists and messages. We use a stick-on white board on our refrigerator door to list what needs to be purchased, messages for each other and notes of what needs to be done with the children, urgent jobs, and so on. The stick-on white board was obtained from a business stationer.

Another way is to use a diary for the family in which everyone writes down their various needs (with the deadline dates attached) to help all the members fit in with one another's schedules and demands. This can work well if people are able to give notice about being away, requiring special meals, needing new clothes or camping equipment or organising transportation.

2 ARE YOU A RISK-TAKER?

Survival tactics and risk-taking

In order to take advantage of opportunities you need to be able to take risks. One aspect of risk-taking relates to gambling and investing substantial amounts of money. On another scale women are often adept at handling money, and it is only when this skill is translated to a larger scale that some women feel inadequate. If one of your new goals is to learn more about handling money, you may have to risk appearing stupid by asking basic questions of people who are already familiar with the wider financial system. Or it could mean risking being insistent that you want to understand some of the financial mysteries presently handled by others in your life.

Risk-taking may mean understanding and involving yourself in how your family (and business) finances work. Of course we can handle financial matters just as well as men. But men have often sought to shield us from the possible dangers involved in taking financial risks.

Recently I was the only woman in a group of five experienced business people helping another woman who was developing plans for her new business.

Thelma had already run her business part-time and had done well over a couple of years even though she was barely 20. Her business plan was directed at making her business a full-time operation. When we discussed it with her it became obvious that she needed to work out a simple forecast of what her costs would be over the year on a month-by-month basis. To my surprise the men in the group suggested she might get a man to do this for her. *They suggested calling on her father or her boyfriend for assistance.*

It was an obvious example of men thinking that a 20-year-old woman was not able to handle her own financial affairs. They were not allowing her to come to grips with understanding her own business or acquiring valuable financial skills.

I was adamant that she do all the figures for the forecast herself if she wished to understand how her business worked and take control of it from the start. In fact, she was quite capable of doing this and at the next meeting presented a well-prepared set of figures.

Quite often this 'protective' shielding of women from the cold, hard world of finance is assumed by institutions as well as individuals as the right stance to adopt. Only gradually are banks and building societies prepared to listen to women speaking independently when they ask for a loan or wish to understand more about their finances.

Penelope Russianoff suggests in her book, *Why Do I Think I Am Nothing Without A Man?*, that women often think that by remaining virginal in financial matters they will remain more attractive to men.[1] If this is so it can be tragic for women who are suddenly left to manage their own finances. Abundant examples of women being ill-prepared to manage their day-to-day finances occur where a husband dies or there is a divorce.

Elsie's story illustrates what can so often happen to women. I discovered her inexperience in money matters a few years ago when she and her husband went north for an extended holiday.

In the years when she had worked she had been used to handling her own money for house-keeping which she managed through her personal savings account. Once she retired, her account was pretty bare.

Her husband had always handled the family bills and finances. He also handled their pension cheques now that they were both retired. She was already well aware of her dependence on him financially and the problems this could cause.

Recently her husband died. Naturally in her grief she

turned to her son to help her sort out her affairs, but she took on the job of paying the various bills, including the funeral expenses. As part of this, the payment to the funeral parlour was the first cheque she had ever signed in her life. I admired her ability to begin to learn, even relatively late, and risk appearing a fool at the bank when she filled in the wrong sections of the form.

The assumption that the man is responsible for paying the household accounts not only makes it difficult for women to take independent financial risks but also leaves them vulnerable as credit risks once they have to fend for themselves. Norma's story shows us how aware we need to be of financial matters.

Norma had several credit cards which she used often when shopping. When she decided to go into her own business her suppliers asked her for credit references. Her credit cards were not regarded as credit references because the accounts had initially been opened by her husband and her cards were supplementary ones which still operated on his account.

Ironically, she had a separate bank account which could have given her access to a credit card in her own name. But because she had assumed the cards were issued jointly she had never bothered obtaining her own.

Just deciding to handle your own money matters may be a big risk-taking event for a woman. But risk-taking goes far beyond money.

Risk-taking may endanger our security

As well as associating risk with gambling and investing we often link it to personal danger.

This kind of risk-taking is most often associated with a male image. Traditionally men have gone to war, climbed ragged peaks, explored primordial forests, rescued lost walkers and sailed around the world in boats. They still go to the Antarctic, and play football.

Of course women can do all these 'dangerous' things just as men can. But again men have sought to 'protect' women from risk-taking in these male-dominated fields. This protective attitude has helped maintain the status quo. It has also resulted in many women not learning any risk-taking skills. For some, it has also resulted in an over-dependence on boyfriends, families, husbands or friends, making it even more difficult for a woman to break away and seize an opportunity.

It is easy to protect children – and women – so that they never take risks and do not learn necessary skills for survival. This can apply to social skills or skills in climbing or taking a chance and appearing a fool. It means that people – male and female – are always encouraged to favour the secure and familiar and are afraid of trying something new.

The risks involved in changing our behaviour, being adventurous, leaving the familiar, feeling lonely, getting hurt, being noticed, being laughed at, trying new things and being different are just as real as the risks we connect with danger and gambling.

The following exercise will encourage you to think about taking risks. It is designed to help you find your current risk-taking level – and discover whether you wish to extend that level in the future.

EXERCISE
Your risk-taking potential (so far)
I suggest you do this exercise twice because it will probably illustrate to you the difference between what you once were capable of risking and how you take risks at present.

For your first attempt tick any of the statements which apply to your life over the last year or so. In some of the sections you may tick one or all of them.

For your second attempt tick any statement which you feel has applied to you at any point of your life.

Pay particular attention to your earlier experiences,

especially if in the last few years you have looked after a family, built a relationship or cared for sick or dependent friends or relatives.

Sometimes it is surprising, and very encouraging, for us to remember how adventurous we were, or might have been before we were temporarily overwhelmed with looking after a home and family, became involved in a relationship or were forced by circumstances to expend our energy caring for others.

1 Eating
a   I prefer plain food with few variations.
b   I enjoy trying different foods occasionally.
c   I often cook a new recipe for meals.
d   I enjoy trying restaurants or shops which serve food from other countries.

2 Hairdos
a   I always have my hair done the same way.
b   I have tried a different haircut or gone to a different hairdresser.
c   I have recently chosen a new style for my hair.
d   I have recently tried out an unusual rinse or had tips done or a very different blow-dry or perm for my hair.

3 Clothes and jewellery
a   I prefer my conservative clothes all the time.
b   I occasionally wear something different or fashionable for fun.
c   I experiment with different outfits to suit different moods or situations or choose my individual style of dress.
d   I enjoy wearing a variety of clothes including unusual outfits or clothes I have designed myself.

ARE YOU A RISK-TAKER?

4 Holidays
a I always go to the same place or do the same thing for my holidays.
b I sometimes go to a different place for a change.
c I look forward to developing new interests or experiencing different things on my holidays or travel overseas.
d I look for adventure, strange places or exciting new situations on a holiday.

5 Living places
a I prefer to remain in the same place.
b I have lived in several different flats or houses in the same area or city or town.
c I have lived in various places or interstate.
d I have lived in different countries.

6 Interests and hobbies
a I have few interests or hobbies at present.
b I have continued the same interests and hobbies as when I was young.
c I have developed and expanded my earlier interests and hobbies into new areas.
d I have taken up new interests and hobbies.

7 Friendships and relationships
a I have kept the same friends I had as a child.
b I have met several new friends at work or through groups or at other places.
c I have joined a different club or group or course to meet new friends.
d I look for new friends among our neighbours or among parents at school or playgroup or through clubs and organisations.

8 Travelling alone
a I do not like going on any trip alone.

- **b** I go on short trips in the car or on public transport by myself.
- **c** I have driven for several days by myself or gone for several days on a trip by bus, train, plane or ship.
- **d** I have gone on extended holidays or tours for weeks or months by myself by car, train, bus, plane, camel, horse, ship, hitch-hiking or walking.

9 Managing financial affairs
- **a** I prefer someone else to pay the bills and manage my investments for me.
- **b** I manage the household money and try to work out a budget.
- **c** I run a cheque account, pay our bills and check the bank statements.
- **d** I look for investment information and manage my own investments.

10 Finding out information
- **a** I listen to a talk or lecture but wait for others to ask questions.
- **b** I try to find out about information or questions I do not understand from books or printed articles.
- **c** I ask people I know to help me or refer me to others who can help me with information when I need it.
- **d** I ask a speaker or lecturer questions in which I am interested or questions about things I have not understood at question time or during the lecture.

11 Changing jobs
- **a** I do not like my job but I will stay there hoping something will change or turn up or improve.
- **b** I keep looking in the job advertisements and have applied for a couple of positions but have not heard anything further.

c I am definitely seeking a new job by telling friends I am keen to move or asking my employer for a new position or answering and following up any likely positions I hear about or see advertised.
d I am quitting my job anyway and will continue to actively look for other jobs or pursue other interests by approaching directly any firm or organisation which is of interest to me as well as keeping an eye and ear open for suitable jobs in advertisements, through friends and agencies.

12 Expanding your horizons
a I wait to be asked to become a member of any club or organisation.
b I become a member of professional or sporting or hobby organisations which interest me.
c I join the committee of an organisation I am interested in if I am asked or nominated.
d I have volunteered or expressed interest in getting on the committee of a club or group or organisation and would like to hold a key position eventually.

To assess your current capacity to take risks, look at your responses to your second go at this exercise. If your ticks were all (a) answers you have certainly chosen very safe, unadventurous paths for most of your activities. If you have a sprinkling of (b) answers as well, you have moved a little way towards trying to be more adaptive in those areas of your life, but you still choose mainly safe routes. A majority of (c) answers shows much more potential for risk-taking and trying new ideas in those areas. If you scored mostly (d) answers you already have a highly developed capacity for risk-taking.

At times when I have given this exercise to groups of people some protest that you need money to take the options of (c) and (d). That is only so in one or two of these sections. The protest about money probably refers more to people's perceptions of being restricted by current circumstances or to their need for financial security than to their actual capacity to take risks.

Similarly I have had people protest that they always choose their clothes in a certain style, ie the one that 'minimises their hips' or 'flatters their figures'. Again this reflects their preparedness to take risks. Some people's clothes make statements about their lifestyle, their love of colour and unusual design or the fact that they do not care about what people think they should wear. Clothes can certainly say something about our capacity to merge with the crowd or stand out from it – how much attention we are prepared to tolerate when we wear them.

EXERCISE
How to use this risk-taking assessment
This is follow-up action. Record in your own private book what your current answers were to the previous exercise with today's date beside it. Now write down any areas in which you would like to record different answers about your risk-taking ability in, say, a year's time. These could be some of your goals. Refer back to them at a later stage to see if you have improved your risk-taking ability.

Risk-taking and change

Here I should point out that our ability to take risks is often directly linked to our self-confidence. We may have the capacity to take risks but have forgotten how to use it. Or we may choose to behave differently and lead a more conservative life to fit in with new values or other people's expectations.

Elizabeth was a person who had excellent potential as a business-woman. However, she married and accepted a support role as a wife. When her husband died he left her with a business which had limped along for years without being very successful. Elizabeth took it over and put her latent risk-taking ability and business skills to the test. Within a few years she had built it up to be a market leader and was a wealthy woman.

Because she was locked into her role as wife she had never asserted herself in his business and had chosen a conservative route for herself. Once she found herself alone with survival at stake she discovered her potential which resulted in her succeeding to the extent of her dreams.

Women like Elizabeth illustrate the dilemma many face: do we have to lose the man in our lives before we dare to take risks and fulfil our potential? Many women still make the 'safe' choice of a support role to a partner but others are trying to achieve both relationships and the fulfillment of ambition.

Some of us may have been badly hurt in the past by people or events. As a result we may have withdrawn to protect ourselves from being hurt again. This often comes out in what we say we cannot do or dislike or are afraid of doing.

What are your fears and dislikes?

We all have fears or dislikes whether they are mild or severe. These fears can form barriers to what we might do with our lives. They restrict our risk-taking ability in those areas. Sometimes they become taboos for us. Ask yourself the following questions:
- Are you afraid of being alone?
- Do you fear heights?
- Do you dislike sewing?
- Do you avoid driving far by yourself?
- Do you avoid driving along winding or rough roads?
- Are you afraid of being thought untidy or dirty?
- Are you afraid of maths?
- Do you dislike going to the toilet in a strange place?

- Do you hate getting dirty or untidy?
- Do you dislike being in uncomfortable accommodation?
- What other strong fears or dislikes do you have?

Some people's views of success are hampered by anxiety. If you are one of these people you must conquer your fear in order to do things that you consider important.

When I hear people insisting they cannot do something which puzzles or worries them, I suggest that something happened in their past to discourage them. Unfortunately, women have often been discouraged more than they have been encouraged to be creative or ambitious.

A common source of discouragement is the teacher, relative or friend who makes us feel a failure. This can happen very easily when we are children, vulnerable and eager to learn and to please. As girls we are usually expected to conform, obey and gain approval for what we do. Boys may be allowed more license to question the orders or to even be untidy.

Illeana had learnt to expect success and to be given approval. Yet she is also an example of how we often learn from childhood to avoid the painful experiences we have had and also to cut off sources of satisfaction.

When I spoke to her she stressed the fact that she could not sew. She insisted that she could not even sew on a button. She did not need to; she could afford to buy all her family's clothing and to pay skilled people to make them if necessary.

I was intrigued that not having this skill still seemed important to her in some way. When I suggested that she must have had a bad experience with it in her early life she described how at school her sewing teacher had thought so little of her ability that she had failed the subject. She believed that her teacher had acted out of spite. The shock had been enough to turn her away from sewing because she associated it with her first failure in life.

The fact that she cannot sew is still of concern to her because she discusses it at such length to justify why she is a failure at it.

The challenge of proving them wrong

Illeana's situation is one which a different type of person would accept as a challenge. For them the possibility of becoming an excellent, perhaps prize-winning, craftswoman would be a spur to conquer the earlier failure. Some of the sense of success would come from proving the teacher wrong. She would prove to herself and to others that she could do it.

This attitude of proving you can do it, particularly to yourself, is important if you want to learn to take risks and overcome past failures. I encounter it often when talking to women who are afraid of, or feel they are not any good at, mathematics. I was so interested in this hang-up which many women seemed to have with the subject that I developed a special course to tackle the problem. As part of the course, I encourage women to write a personal maths history. Like Illeana many are able to pinpoint the exact year or teacher or situation in their lives where their confidence in being able to do maths crumbled. Some of them are astonished to realise that in primary school they had been excellent at maths and had enjoyed it. Many then go on to conquer their fear of the subject.

Comfort versus discomfort

Taking risks can mean getting hurt because it involves changing our lives and what we have been comfortable with. Also, trying to challenge fears and dislikes, meeting new people and working out new ideas makes us vulnerable. Change can be very uncomfortable to live with, especially in the beginning.

Deciding how uncomfortable we can bear to feel will greatly affect our decisions about seizing opportunities and directing our own lives. What may strike us at first is that finding new friends we can trust and feel comfortable with is not easy. Many of the people we meet may have other values or ideas. Also we may gradually realise that our needs in a relationship now are different from those we had earlier in our lives. We may have to adapt our approach to people if we want to get on with them in a new way.

We may realise that the paths we want to follow are unusual and call for action rather than friendship. This realisation may give us a different basis to meet and work with people – a basis that does not place such high emphasis on intimacy, but rather enables us to use people's skills and ability and learn from their experience as we work alongside them to reach our objectives. This may in fact lead to us being more tolerant.

All of this involves change and taking risks with people and new situations. How can we learn to do it? Increasing our self-confidence is a key.

Self-confidence

Building self-confidence is a long-term job. I think of it as a life-time task. Most of us find that when we face new situations or crises we suddenly falter, even though we may usually feel very confident. The skills we have learnt can help us to overcome these feelings of inadequacy but we need to encourage ourselves continually.

Often we look back after a few years and realise how our confidence has grown. What was nerve-racking for us in the beginning has now become familiar, even enjoyable. However it is also a chicken-and-egg process. We all have to start somewhere. Then the more we take risks and congratulate ourselves for daring to direct our lives, the more confident we become.

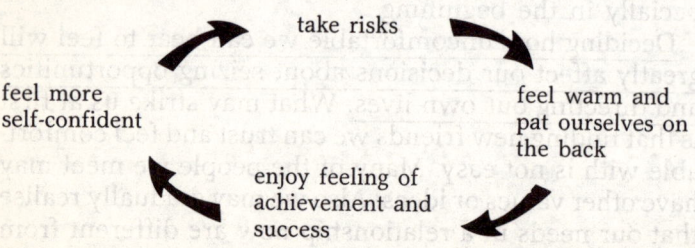

Consider Eva who joined a committee and enjoyed working in the small group. Because she was enthusiastic she was elected president after a couple of years. Although she felt confident and comfortable in small committee meetings she found that having to address regular dinners of large groups of members very daunting.

To help her feel more confident at first, she planned carefully and wrote down everything she intended to say. She also spoke into a tape recorder and listened to herself so that she could find out how she needed to improve her delivery.

She still felt extremely nervous at her first dinner. She could eat very little, and was glad when her speech was over. Thanks to her preparation she spoke very adequately and concealed her nervousness. After doing this several times she began to feel more relaxed about addressing these gatherings. She still planned what to say but could now do it in note form. She could also enjoy her meal.

By the end of the year she realised that she was quite confident in addressing large groups. She was even beginning to enjoy it.

Reflecting on what we have done in the past can be very encouraging when we are facing changes in our lives and find them overwhelming, frightening or simply difficult to face.

Realising that we have taken risks in the past can reassure us of our capacity to do so again. Even when we are tired and weighed down for a while with pressures of family or work or both, we do not lose the capacity to take risks. This is something about which we can remind ourselves, and fall back on to restore our self-confidence once we are ready to go on to the next stage of our development.

Ways to help us take risks

Some of the ways which can help us to cope with our fears before we take risks are to:

ARE YOU A RISK-TAKER?

- pre-plan
- collect information
- decide on strategies.

Here are some examples that may help you.

Pre-plan
- Decide to get there early to avoid getting hassled, particularly if it is a new place or situation. You can then choose to seat yourself where you will be most at ease.
- Decide which outfit you will wear to feel comfortable, attractive and self-confident.
- If you have children, organise a babysitter a couple of days in advance so you will not lose the courage to go to the meeting that night.
- Cook a new dish for a visitor rather than your family.

Collect information
- Talk to friends about a new hairdresser before you try them out.
- Collect free travel brochures from the travel agent.
- Read a magazine about new clothes.
- Borrow an informative cookbook from the local library before you try a new cuisine.
- Find out from local libraries about a variety of local interests and hobby groups.
- Ring up an information centre; for example those that are often provided by women's information services in government departments.

Strategy decisions
- Decide to ask one question in your class today about something you do not understand.
- Decide what you will eat for your three meals today to avoid putting on weight.
- Ask if a friend or relative is interested in joining a group or at least in going to a meeting with you.
- If you know no-one at a meeting or conference decide

to go up and talk to a particular person who spoke up or raised a question on a topic which interested you.

Risk-taking and survival: other women's views

Overcoming fear enables us to become better at taking risks. Often this means learning to appear calm and confident even when we are like jelly underneath. Finding out how others feel and knowing that most people experience the same anxieties, is encouraging. We are not alone.

For my own survival I have found taking deep breaths very calming before I ask questions in public or make a comment at an important meeting. This slows down my heart palpitations and stops that annoying and embarrassing lump in my throat that used to make my voice break when I was about to speak.

Natasha Josefowitz says in *Paths to Power*:

'Of course, what is a risk for you may not be a risk for someone else, and vice versa. You know when you are taking a risk by the signals your body gives you. I get a knot in the pit of my stomach and a tightness in my throat. If I'm standing with a paper in my hand, the paper will shake, so I try to place papers on solid surfaces. If I am sitting, I have learned not to lean forward, but to lean back so that I feel anchored against my seat. If I'm standing up, I try to walk back and forth and not look too paralyzed.'[2]

Taboos

Finally, you might consider whether you are fettered unconsciously by taboos. Taboos are the restrictions we often carry around in our subconscious. Therefore, often we do not realise they are there.

Taboos may stop us from doing things differently because we were brought up as children to do them in a certain way. Or we may have established our own taboos by fixing patterns of behaviour that had a purpose at the time but have now become irrelevant.

Part of your action plan may mean re-examining your taboos or rules in order to be more flexible to meet changes in your life. For example, are you still following someone else's ideas of how clean a house has to be? Does this limit your time to relax or develop other interests? Maybe the taboo says that you have to make the beds and clean up the kitchen every day before you leave the house. What would happen if you broke it? Are you able to change your style of housework to suit your circumstances? During holidays do you still demand a spotless home to the detriment of your relaxation and your family's fun?

Are you able to adjust your efforts as you get older to suit your own wishes? I think of the very independent 86-year-old mother who wrote triumphantly to her daughter that she had at last left her bed unmade in case she might want to get back into it after she had hosed the garden, made a cake or washed her dishes.

Do you have taboos about your image of what women should and should not do which stop you from doing something you might enjoy having a go at because it might be considered 'unlady like'? Are you a frustrated welder or plumber at heart?

Do you have a taboo about wearing clothes which are a little unusual because they might not be thought to suit you? Are you following society's image or authoritative opinions on how you should always stick to plain colours or small prints or up-and-down stripes because they 'flatter' you?

Do you believe that phoning a man for a date is unacceptable? Or that as a wife you should always wait for your husband to make the first move? These are old taboos. To challenge them, to take the risk in doing so, may bring you a great sense of control and freedom.

Give yourself a chance. Let go of your taboos. Take time to appreciate the joy of life around you. Life is too short to miss out on experiences because of taboos. Take hold of your life and do it today.

3 IS THAT ALL THERE IS TO LIFE?

Unlocking your potential

Most people have unrealised potential – qualities they have not yet developed. Many women can begin to unlock their potential and still maintain their family life with minimal disruption. Others know that choosing to develop their potential will lead to changes on the domestic front; they may have to decide how to cope with different situations. This chapter as well as Chapters Eight, 10 and 12 discuss methods which may assist you if this is your situation.

Sometimes the need to develop our potential comes at a point we remember keenly. Sometimes it is a gradual change and development. We recognise that it has happened only years later when we look back and compare things as they are now with the way they used to be.

I still remember hanging baby clothes on the line and thinking to myself: 'And I went to university for this?'. That was eight years ago.

The realisation led me to seek ways of earning enough money to pay someone else to do the house-cleaning and washing. I then finished a diploma, spent more time working in our business and started going to meetings of various professional groups. My career developed from that point.

Betty Friedan spoke about it in her book, *The Feminine Mystique:*

'The problem lay buried, unspoken for many years, in the minds of American women. It was a strange stirring, a sense of dissatisfaction... Each suburban wife struggled with it alone. As she made the beds, shopped for groceries, matched slipcover material, ate peanut butter sandwiches with her children, chauffeured Cub Scouts and Brownies, lay beside her husband at night – she was afraid to ask even of herself the silent question – "Is this all?".'[1]

Colette Dowling describes it in her book, *The Cinderella Complex:*

'How, when you had dared nothing in life, do you begin to dare? What gives you the little push, the impetus to move out to the edge of what's familiar and step off? For many women it is a feeling of despair.'

'When I began, finally, to write, it was not at school, not at *Mademoiselle*, but in a little five-roomed railroad flat just north of Greenwich Village, when my second baby was a month old. I remember the night so clearly, for in no way had I anticipated what was to happen. The rush had come from nowhere (or so it seemed on hindsight) – a sudden, compelling urge to write, to put down words on paper... It was glorious and focused, the first utterly independent experience I'd had since marrying.'[2]

So if you have had the feeling that there has to be more to life than you are experiencing at present, feel reassured. Others have felt the feeling and done something about it.

Feeling depressed

Most people have felt depressed at some period of their lives even if it was only for a short time. I believe that feeling depressed for extended periods may be due to various causes and that while unpleasant, depression can have very positive aspects. It often acts as a goad or signpost directing us towards change. It also often marks the beginning of a new and creative era, particularly if we accept it and try to understand the causes.

Seeking professional help

If you are seriously depressed there is great benefit in talking to a therapist. Some depression can only be helped through the skills of a trained therapist. Professional assistance is often the turning-point which enables people to cope with life once more on their own terms and be enthusiastic about the future.

If you find that the next few sections are very relevant to you but that you cannot manage these kind of personal changes on your own, seeking therapy could be a vital first step. It will speed up the process of getting back in touch with yourself in order to enjoy living and start really exploring those opportunities which at present are hidden from you.

Depression: a reaction to crises

One of the common causes of depression is our reaction to the grief of losing our close friends, family or relatives. Another is our reaction to crises when we are uprooted from our homes or countries or find we suddenly have been abandoned to fend for ourselves through a separation, divorce or death.

If we find ourselves depressed because of one of these situations we should allow ourselves the chance to recover from such a crisis. We need to be gentle with ourselves, because time is indeed a great healer.

One positive view of depression is that it offers an excellent chance for us to evaluate our lives before going on to the next stage. You might find that this is constructive in helping you to face a new life alone if your grief is due to a divorce or break-up in a relationship or the death of a close relative or friend. Becoming depressed might, however, also reflect our repressed emotions of anger or resentment or fear which we need to recognise and sort out before we can go on to the next stage of our lives.

Depression and PMT

Fortunately depression is now a well recognised symptom of pre-menstrual tension. We can do something about it once we realise that it stems from our bodies and not the psyche.

If you find you feel depressed every few weeks for a couple of days and then pick up again, check how it fits in with your monthly periods. If the pattern corresponds you can then explore options to help you cope with it.

There are various books now available on the subject. A useful one is *PMT The Unrecognised Illness*.[3] It provides an appendix on 'Where to Get Help' which lists places for women to go to for further assistance.

Depression: a chemical reaction

One of the lesser known causes of depression is our body's reactions to chemicals within our system. These reactions can cause physical and mental changes which we might not initially link with chemicals. The foods you eat and the substances you come in contact with may cause various reactions to your body. We are fairly familiar with allergies, hay fever and skin rashes as symptoms of these reactions. However, becoming depressed may also be a reaction.

Although most of the research conducted on this has concentrated on children's allergies, anyone can suffer from an intolerance to a particular food or chemical.

If you suspect that you are affected by particular foods or situations or even medications you ought to explore whether this is connected to depression. Either a medical specialist or naturopath can test you.

Depression: a symptom of powerful emotions

For many women feeling depressed can be a symptom of anger at their level of existence. When we begin to get in touch with ourselves we may recognise that we are feeling angry, powerless, repressed, caged in, imprisoned, jealous, inadequate, resentful, helpless, unfulfilled, bored, walked over. Do any of these seem to fit with the way you feel?

If you are depressed it can be useful to try to work out what emotions you are experiencing. Women often feel depressed because they lack self-esteem. We feel inadequate and lacking in confidence. We often receive very little encouragement from partners, family and friends. We doubt our worth not only to ourselves but to others.

Feeling depressed can be a signal to us to begin to change the way we live. We can then begin to grow as individuals and begin to look at different tracks to follow and new challenges to pursue.

Building our self-talk

Our level of self-esteem has a lot to do with the way we talk to ourselves. And we are the ones who decide what we say to ourselves and whether we will listen or not. Taking control over our lives can begin by deciding to change just those things we say to ourselves. When we feel depressed these messages or self-talk can become our survival tactics.

Patting ourselves on the back for the ordinary things we do and being patient with ourselves can be very cheering. Telling ourselves that we are not stupid, that we are capable and can do things in our own special way begins to lift our spirits.

While on this point I believe it is important to squelch the common 'put-down' banter that a family often has developed towards the wife and mother. Too often that banter becomes what we say about ourselves both internally and to others. Muttering to ourselves 'Gosh, you're stupid today! Why did you do that?' is not a positive way to regard oneself. As a person who runs a house seven days a week you are entitled to have bad days and get things muddled sometimes. But that does not make you stupid. Phrases like 'silly old Mum' may not sound very serious but they can become part of the image the family develops of you which reinforces your own low self-image at a time when you really need some genuine praise for the job you do in running the household.

A no-nonsense cutting out of such put-downs can be a worthwhile way to start changing your own image in your eyes and in those of your family. Then you can start forgiving yourself for the muddled days and encouraging yourself for anything you have achieved – which may often mean simply surviving with or without dignity – especially if you have young children.

I can still remember when I first started to use this positive patting on the back for myself. Both the children were very young and I had arranged to have a picnic lunch with a friend. I had worked hard in the morning to preserve the peace and still get a minimal degree of order into the kitchen, organise the baby's milk and pack a picnic. As I went to pick up the mail I thought to myself, 'You are doing well, Margaret'. And I still remember smiling and feeling a sense of happiness which really cheered me up and enabled me to enjoy the rest of the day.

It takes effort to change how we talk to ourselves. But we <u>can</u> change. And the effort to change begins to give us control over our lives. We <u>can</u> learn to stop running ourselves down or comparing ourselves negatively with others. Of course this self-talk idea is another chicken-and-egg routine.

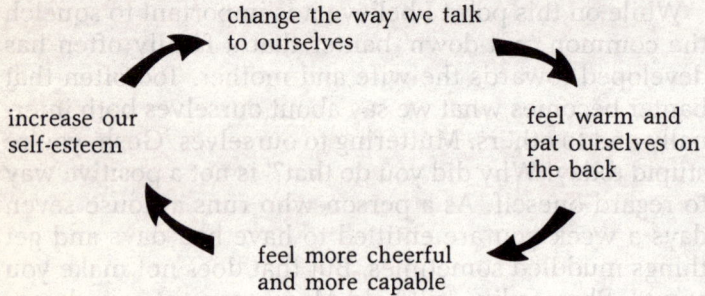

It often helps to write down how we feel about things. You could do this in your personal book as a record of your progress. Just write it down as you feel it. No-one else will read it. Even key words can release our emotions and help us to understand how we are really feeling about things. I have found that keeping records you can look back on can be very encouraging in helping you to recognise how far you have progressed in your own development. You then have even more reason to pat yourself on the back and keep on going.

Baring your soul to nature

Another avenue worth exploring is to begin to open up your soul to some of the minor events of living. It is so easy to lose sight of simple pleasures especially when you bear the responsibility of many burdens. And the great thing about them is that they are free.

One of the simple pleasures we can all share is the changing face of nature. For example, we often spend much time developing gardens. How long is it since you actually sat in a garden and simply opened your mind to absorbing and enjoying its beauty? Even a single superb flower or a tree in blossom can be mind-blowing if we allow ourselves the time to observe it, let it flow through our senses and touch our inner being. Or you may enjoy a day bush-walking or sitting by a waterfall. When can you do this again?

How long is it since you sat and listened to the forest around you? Or found a beach and walked along with the waves? Or simply lay down on a bench or rug in the sun and let the warmth soak through you?

The changing of seasons is a constant wonder which we may sometimes become too bound up in life to appreciate. Some years ago when the children were young I decided to deliberately re-train myself to absorb these wonders and appreciate them. I started by going out to sit on a bench in the garden after tea while the children were watching television. This gave me a guaranteed half-hour of solitude.

It took a bit of practice gradually to turn off the cares of the day, unwind from the tensions and open my eyes to colours of the sunset, trees in blossom, autumn leaves or the new greenness of spring buds. The magic of dusk is elusive unless we lift our heads from the bench or sink and go out to meet it.

Gradually as I learnt to relax and enjoy it I found my half-hour absorbing the atmosphere of the changing twilight in the garden a healing process.

Learning to appreciate the momentary pleasures around us is a lasting way to refresh our souls. One night I rushed into the supermarket late to buy essential provisions for our evening meal. I felt harried as I came out of the doors, thinking about which child I had to pick up from which friend before I returned home. I was totally unprepared for the fact that twilight had crept up while I was in the supermarket. As I walked across the car park I found the evening sky breathtaking. The sky combined a rare palette of colours ranging from the last rose streaks of the sunset to deepening navy with several early stars and a crescent moon. I took time to absorb and enjoy the scene over the supermarket car park and I smiled with pleasure. Then I was able to face the tasks of family and dinner with equanimity. My inner soul was unexpectedly refreshed.

These are the experiences we often need to remember when we are faced with changes in our lives.

Change and feelings

When we talked about risk-taking I mentioned that change can be uncomfortable to live with. I want to discuss this idea in more detail. Changing things becomes easier as they become habits for us even though doing things differently may feel unfamiliar at first.

The idea of giving ourselves positive messages of encouragement, hope and acceptance may not be comfortable in the beginning. But as we learn to listen to ourselves, the habit becomes more familiar.

Many of us already use these established methods to change the behaviour of our children or people with whom we work. We are used to giving praise even when there may be only a scrap of reason to do so in order to build up a child's precious self-esteem.

In our lives and work we often comfort others and encourage them to try again when things have worked out differently from what they hoped and expected. Now we have to remember to do that for ourselves too.

Even though deciding to take action can be encouraging for us, this process of trying new things is not always comfortable. That is where there is often a difference between a logical decision and an emotional response to it. The logical decision is generally made and acted on before we can accept the situation emotionally. This especially happens when our self-esteem has been low. Allowing ourselves to relax enough to enjoy new experiences can take time. We are often too busy feeling self-conscious.

When we really want to change we can gradually learn to attempt new ways of doing things as the first step, learn to be comfortable and confident later and ultimately enjoy the changes.

We can recognise the steps we need to work through in changing anything as:
- deciding to change
- acting to change
- becoming familiar with the situation
- becoming confident and relaxed
- feeling enjoyment or contentment.

The following example shows how one woman reacted when she made changes to her life.

Yvonne decided to enrol in a course at a college. She had not studied since leaving school and was very anxious about this new situation. On her first day she got lost and was late for the first lecture. When she eventually arrived she fought back her tears and tried to concentrate on what the lecturer was saying.

For the first week she felt an absolute stranger in the college. She forced herself to go to each lecture and found herself jostled in the crowded corridors. Even in the canteen it took her days before she could decide on what she wanted and ask confidently for it.

The first assignment was a nightmare. She agonised over what it meant and how she could ever get it done. She decided to ask one of the other students about it. The student was very glad to have someone else to talk things over with. They worked on the assignment together and began to build up a friendship.

When Yvonne found that she had passed her first assignment she felt very pleased. After that she gradually began to get used to the college with its different ways. She made a few friends and by the end of the first term she realised she was actually looking forward to returning there after the holidays. What had started as an ordeal had become familiar and even enjoyable.

Fitness and relaxation

Besides talking positively to ourselves in order to raise our self-esteem we can also add to our mental and physical being by exercising.

Exercise is very relaxing. It begins to break down the tension that being depressed generates in your body. If you are feeling depressed, doing relaxing, enjoyable exercise can put your mind into neutral and relieve the pressures you are feeling.

I have found that deciding to exercise regularly and becoming fit has been a turning-point in helping me to recover from being depressed. Over a number of years I have changed from being a person who enjoyed walking but did very little other exercise to someone who now regularly swims and goes for bike rides. In between I have done exercises at home, enjoyed aerobics classes, and discovered the delights of saunas and massage.

I learnt to ride a bike on the local bike track when my daughter got hers and we decided to invest in bikes for Mum and Dad as well. Now I find great satisfaction in riding up hills and becoming more skilled on the machine. Not only am I fitter but I feel more self-confident knowing the success I have had in learning a new skill. Both are important elements in ridding oneself of depression.

When you start to exercise choose something which you will enjoy and which will give you the satisfaction of achievement once you have been doing it for a short time. The possibilities are many. Go for a long walk rather than drive the car. Walk up stairs rather than take the lift or escalator. Or start your own regular exercises at home. (An excellent source is the Canadian Airforce book on 5BX and 10BX graded exercises for men and women.)

If you have children take the opportunity of playing cricket, badminton, tennis or ball with them. One of the ways I have kept close to my son has been through playing cricket with him on summer evenings. Sometimes when I have started reluctantly I have been surprised at how quickly I have enjoyed the experience.

If you are interested in other sports look around for a social club or association. Most neighbourhoods have tennis, squash and bowls groups who meet regularly if you are interested in this type of exercise. It can also provide you with a new group of friends. Or you may prefer to join a class to do aerobic exercises, jazz ballet, yoga or meditation. As part of relaxing consider using facilities at a sports' centre or gym to have a sauna, a spa or even a massage. These are often available at public facilities like universities, colleges or local councils as well as in commercial fitness centres.

<u>If you choose to try something new be gentle with yourself.</u> It is important you give yourself time to develop new skills and not allow the learning to be frustrating. There is no point doing an exercise which makes you feel more depressed if you do not succeed at it after a reasonable effort.

Losing weight later
You need to feel very positive and like yourself a great deal before you are able seriously to change your eating habits. When you start talking positively to yourself you might also begin to forgive yourself for being fat. Once

you are doing more exercise you will probably lose some weight anyway. Do not expect to lose weight and change your behaviour at the same time. Again, be gentle with yourself.

What you can expect is that at some time in the future when you are talking positively to yourself and feeling very self-confident and assured, then you will be able to decide to change your eating habits because it becomes important to you to do so. And you will then be able to do it and succeed just as you have found success in other ways.

EXERCISE
What you might begin to change

This exercise is designed to encourage you to make more space in which to do the things you enjoy. One way to achieve this is to recognise how you feel about your life. Then you can decide which bits you might try to rearrange or change.

To do this exercise effectively you need to <u>be honest with yourself</u>. After all, this is your own <u>private book</u>. No-one need ever know what you write in it. Start the list now and come back to it as you remember more things you want to add. Write down all the things you can think of that you do or would like to do at present.

Your list might look a bit like this:

cooking	starting a business
ironing	putting out the garbage
writing	going to the beach
doing housework	family outings
playing music	joining a jazz group
earning money	making cakes
visiting relatives	going to the ballet
studying	typing
using a computer	shopping by myself

IS THAT ALL THERE IS TO LIFE?

cleaning up the kitchen
taking the children to the park
playing sport
joining a group
getting a part-time job
being active in a theatre group
looking after the children by myself
working
visiting friends
staying home at night by myself
swimming
eating out as a family
watching TV
going out to dinner
entertaining friends
learning to play a musical instrument
doing aerobics
playing with children
having a barbecue
gardening
composing music
sewing
looking for a job
working with other people
doing community work
reading
going out to a film
buying my own records
fishing
learning a craft
looking after the pets
talking to friends
doing a craft, and so on.

Now sort them into two columns according to how you feel. If you are neutral about some put them in a third column or leave them out.

_____ I enjoy _____ I hate _____

Now you can put marks beside them. Start with the easy ones – the 'I enjoy' column. Put an asterisk (*) beside any of the things you would like to do more often or maybe start doing again. Put an exclamation mark (!) beside any of the things you would enjoy doing early in the day if you left your chores till later.

Select which of these enjoyable activities you intend to indulge in more often. Write down when you will start doing them and how often. Check after a week to see how many you have given more time to.

Now you can mark the 'I hate' column. Put a cross (x) beside any of those things which you could:
- stop doing altogether
- delegate to someone else
- do less of
- refuse to do
- trade, swap or share
- pay someone else to do.

Creative thinking: how to change
Here are some possible ways of approaching the 'I hate' items. Which ones would you like to try out?

The reward method
The idea here is to decide to do today's necessary tasks quickly so that you can reward yourself with something you enjoy doing later.

The delay method
Here the idea is to spend time now on doing what you enjoy and allow yourself the minimum time necessary to do urgent tasks later by a deadline.

The random choice method
If you are inclined to gamble you can put the various tasks you want done today in a jar and pick them out one at a time. When you have finished that one you can pick the next one, and so on.

The delegate method
This may begin to start challenging your accepted pattern of living by thinking of what tasks your partner, children, father, mother, neighbour or friend could do for you either regularly or occasionally.

Making it work requires a decision to discuss the matter with the people involved, to get their agreement or to place the responsibility for the tasks squarely on their shoulders.

The trade-off method
Here you decide what items you would like someone else to do. Then you agree on something you are prepared to do, give up or take on in return.

You are in a better position of controlling your life if you can think of what to offer in return before you raise the matter. But sometimes there is a good basis for negotiation if both parties work out together what they are prepared to do for the other.

You do not need to change everything straight away. Decide to try one or two things which are important to you. Then pat yourself on the back for trying to change.

Finally do not be discouraged if you do not succeed the first time. Pick something else and try again.

Action points
Write down the things you can cut out doing altogether by delegating, trading or paying someone else to do. Then write down how you plan to make the changes and include the date by which you intend to have acted on the decision.

Here are some examples. You may decide to spend an hour at your favourite hobby tomorrow while your toddler sleeps. You may give yourself a week to explore with your neighbours when and how to share an afternoon a week looking after each other's children. You may give yourself till after the weekend to work out what trade-off you can make with your partner so that he or she will cook the meal one night a week or week about or whatever. Give yourself two months to plan a holiday by yourself to somewhere you have always dreamt of, even if your best friend will not come with you.

People have tried these and succeeded

Giving up ironing
Joan put a fold-away ironing board in their bedroom. Whenever she or her husband needs to iron clothes each person irons his or her own things. Joan deliberately buys clothes for herself and the children that need no ironing. She folds clothes as they come off the line or out of the dryer to prevent creasing.

Cutting down on gardening
When Clare and her husband both realised they hated gardening they decided to move to a house with a low-maintenance garden. Now they spend more weekends camping.

Coping with staying home at nights alone with the children
This happens often when both men and women assume that responsibility for looking after children rests with the woman of the house.

Mary found she was tired of being at home at nights while her husband was out studying. She hired a babysitter regularly so that she could go to see friends, go to a movie or the theatre.

Diane decided that having time at night by herself offered her an opportunity to start writing again. She started working on a book and found the time alone after the children were in bed much more productive than when her husband was around.

Rhonda discussed and agreed with her husband which night a week he would stay at home to look after the children. Now she has the opportunity to share a drink or a meal with friends after work and then goes to a night class.

Jane and her husband joined a babysitting co-operative. Now he does some of the babysitting for other members and takes his books to study while he babysits. Jane goes to a meeting of a group she has joined and can call on a babysitter from the co-operative when she needs to.

Studying
Joanne started a course the year her child went to kindergarten. She studied intensively during the hours her child was away and left the housework to do when the child was at home.

Marion started studying while she was pregnant. She took her baby to classes and breast-fed him when necessary in the back row until he was old enough to leave with a friend for a few hours.

Reading
Helen decided to read a book each afternoon while her young children had a rest. Even though this was not easy in the beginning she insisted they play in their rooms to give her time to herself. She eventually established a pattern which left her space to herself to read even when the children grew older.

Sharing the chores
Women often find this very difficult. Even when members of the family agree to do certain tasks they often do them differently from women. This can be frustrating if you insist everything be done to your special standards or methods. The secret is to transfer responsibility to the people undertaking the tasks and learn to relax about how and when they are done. Family members often have to learn how to do things they are unfamiliar with. But remember, there are many ways to do tasks. Seldom is your way the only way.

Rita decided she did not want to do all the cleaning up as well as preparing all the meals. She told her husband she would like him to help clean up after meals. He suggested he was prepared to do that if she could keep their bedroom tidier. But Rita had to realise that her husband might leave the cleaning up till just before he went

IS THAT ALL THERE IS TO LIFE?

to bed. This was not a problem once she got used to walking away from the untidy kitchen. Now they are each happy with the trade-off they reached.

4 WHAT IS THIS THING SUCCESS?

Because people have their own ideas about success I want to start this important chapter with a couple of simple exercises.

These could be some of the most interesting and enlightening exercises you ever do in terms of understanding yourself. You will need undisturbed time for concentration, so allow yourself a couple of hours to do and analyse them because you may find in the beginning that you cannot easily recall what you need to write down.

EXERCISE
Feelings of success
To do these exercises effectively you need to be honest about how you feel. Writing down what first comes to mind is very important. Remember, getting in touch with your own personal feelings is the key to your future.

First, write down several experiences which you feel are the most successful things you have done so far in your life. Secondly, write down several experiences you feel are the least successful.

Now take the obvious sections of your life and write them down. Your choice may be similar to this:
1 Childhood and school days (first 17 years)
2 Leaving school, college, first jobs, and so on (17–20 years)
3 Marriage (twenties)
4 Family (thirties)
5 Forties till now.

You may prefer to add more sections to suit your

> own life pattern. For each of those sections fill in the following information:
>
> Life period   My successes   Why I felt successful
>
> You can write down anything which comes to mind which you associate with success for yourself... which you feel was a success for you then or now... which gives you a warm glow when you think about it.
>
> As part of this exercise you will also think of things you have done which other people might think should be successes for you. Jot them down separately. Later you can analyse why you did not value them as successes.

The following is part of Delia's list.

Life period	Successful Experiences	Reasons why I felt successful
5–20 years	Living in college at university	I proved I could make friends.
20–27 years	Church group	Enjoyed friendship with people of similar interests.
	Tourist visit to a shrine in South America	Made friends on the bus. Enjoyed proving I could do it on my own.
	Working in a foreign country	Success with relationships. Had a chance to test my resources in a different environment.

When Delia went back and looked for patterns she realised two clear factors emerged in her reasons for feel-

ing successful. One of them was satisfying her need for friendship and the other one was her satisfaction in testing her resources when in difficult situations by herself.

She also realised she did not feel successful about being top of her class right through school even though others would assume that was one of her successful experiences.

This suggested to her that the situations she would feel most successful about would be ones where she had friends and/or could use her resources by herself.

She was then able to look for a job which began to offer her some challenge in using her resources but also gave her the opportunity to meet other people and make friends in the work situation. She found this in a research position where she was free to do some work by herself but still be part of a team of people with whom she had common interests.

Why look for success patterns?

People often find that analysing what makes them <u>feel</u> successful reveals much about their past and their present attitudes towards living. These include:

- erratic job histories
- a seeming inability to meet deadlines
- disillusionment with situations where they knew they did well but could not feel any satisfaction from their results
- ambivalent attitudes towards 'achievement'
- a gulf between their attitude and performance at school and college and their later expectations of success
- why 'achievements' in academic or sporting events at school did not count as successes.

The more we recognise how and why we do things, the better we are able to understand our present behaviour and to change it if we wish. As part of taking control of our lives I believe this self-knowledge is vitally important. It is all part of giving ourselves more power, more freedom to choose. How else can we begin to feel we are fulfilling our potential?

Sometimes people are surprised to find out that they have trouble defining specific occasions in their lives when they felt the elation of success. They are further surprised if the occasions are not associated with any of their paid work.

For many of us hobbies or creative situations are the greatest source of feelings of success. For others it may be interacting with people on holidays or on voluntary projects.

Other reasons for feeling successful include:
- learning skills which help overcome fear
- being able to learn something new
- breaking personal established ways of doing things in order to try new ideas
- proving you can do it when others said you could not.

Learning to overcome fear may include building up your self-confidence so that you can cope with new situations, for example deciding to overcome a fear of heights, in order to climb a steep flight of stairs to a magnificent view or an historical site in a Mayan village in Mexico. Being able to learn new skills especially in sport is a source of pride and success for many older women. Learning to swim is a common sporting skill older people achieve and gain pleasure from.

Taking children to lessons may present opportunities for you to increase your skills at the same time, to learn from the same teacher, or simply to make use of the facilities. I always look forward to having a swim and a sauna myself when I take our children for their swimming lessons, especially in the summer holidays.

Perhaps you could do jazz ballet or trampolining or learn a martial art like judo at the same place that your children go for lessons. Learning to ski is another challenge which older women have tackled and found successful.

How to use your success patterns
This emerging insight and self-knowledge about how and why you felt successful in the past can be significant in helping you to decide where you want to go in the future. Basically, it enables you to look for situations which are more in tune with your skills and needs if you find that your current work situation, paid or unpaid, is not bringing you enough satisfaction.

If you realise that you need more scope for creativity, why not open up some part of your life to allow time to pursue that. Or set it as a goal to work towards as soon as you can (see Chapter Five on goals).

You may decide to settle for mundane paid work to bring in necessary income and concentrate on hobbies or part-time experiences to provide the success or achievement element.

Alternatively, you may decide to work for yourself in order to do some of the things you have always wanted to do. Here are some comments by women who run their own small businesses. Extracts are taken from *Minding Your Own Business* by Jo Kinross and Sylvie Shaw.[1]

Helen Medaris had to support five kids when she started her own furniture removal business after managing a similar business for someone else and running a courier service.

'*Some people expect success to happen overnight, but I know it doesn't happen like that. You've got to build up a good relationship with people; your name has to be built up – not just your work, but your name is what's important. And once it is built up, there's no way you'd look back.*

'*You've got to try. I believe you've got to try anything and if you don't succeed, at least you've tried it; if it doesn't work you then have to work on making it work. I enjoy the whole thing, I really do.*'

Hazel Edwards is now a well established author.

'*I always wanted to be a writer, and all my activities were aimed at that. It has given me a sense of purpose.*

WHAT IS THIS THING SUCCESS?

A lot of women, at present, are a bit lost. One way of regaining a sense of identity or purpose is by extending skills. Unfortunately, in our society, unless you are paid for a skill, it tends not to be valued. For that reason, I think it is very important to earn income from whatever it is that you are doing. You need the boost of earning an income, not just for the money, but for the self-confidence associated with economic independence.'

Sharon Wright became a carpenter because she did not really like hairdressing.

'I wanted to become a carpenter mainly because of the challenge. After I have finished a job it is most satisfying. It is like that with anything, even sewing and the traditional jobs I do at home. I just like to see results.'

Golda Schoenbaum runs a business offering bookkeeping and business services.

'I thought, how can I organize myself so that I can earn my living out of what I most like doing, which is staying at home? I realized that I needed a typewriter, so I got a really old second-hand bomb, but it worked, Then I decided to get some cards printed and handed them out to everybody I knew. I placed some advertisements which weren't very successful, but got a few calls, which were encouraging. The rest has been by word of mouth. I won't ever be a tycoon, but I'm living quite well and am happy because I have autonomy over my time, which is what I need most.'

Barbara Pleasance became a spinner and potter after an accident which led to her being dismissed after 14 years as a laboratory technician.

'After losing my job I had a tremendous trauma about meeting other people, but the first thing you notice at the Centre is how warm and friendly everyone is; they want to teach you, they want to relax, and you tend to be very much better for the experience. Going to the Learning Centre has been financially very beneficial for me. Before going to class I didn't think I could earn any money from spinning. I had no idea about it; it was just a desper-

ate measure to learn some form of work with my hands and brain that would take my mind off other problems. We found I could earn money from it and this was marvellous...

'I wouldn't go back to a regular job. The first thing you have to understand is that if you work for yourself you work twice as long and probably twice as hard. However, it does give you a feeling of satisfaction; that you're doing what you want to. You're getting money from people who are delighted with your craft and appreciate the effort you've expended.'

Success is in your mind

I believe success is essentially intangible. It is a bit like wealth and happiness. Success, wealth and happiness mean very different things to different people. We all know stories about people who own immense amounts of money but do not feel happy. They appear to be wealthy in one sense but they have not found the secret of enjoying life and feeling good.

Similarly we can all think of people we know who appeared to have all the ingredients for success when they were young. Maybe they went to school with us, studied with us at college or university, worked with us or lived in our street. But they do not appear to have gained happiness or success. Often to other people we may appear to be wealthy or successful but within ourselves we do not believe it.

Family influence on feeling successful

Our initial feelings about success are directly related to what we were encouraged to feel good about as children. This is often on a subconscious level. Families have values which they use to encourage or discourage children's behaviour. Our neighbours, friends and schools also have values which influence how they accept or reject our behaviour.

The initial feelings we have about many things including success often relate to what we got approval for and were rewarded for when we were children.

We are all aware of the fact that sometimes parents place unrealistic expectations on their children's choice of careers. This sometimes happens when parents themselves had unfulfilled ambitions or aspirations which they hope to see realised through their own children. It can also happen when people want safe, secure careers or good marriages for their daughters.

Girls have often been encouraged to go into teaching as a career. Sally tried teaching but was not happy and left after a few years to start her own business. She was very successful in the business but her parents found it difficult to accept that Sally would prefer to work in her own business than be a respectable teacher with a secure income.

Fortunately Sally had a very supportive husband and friends who gave her the encouragement to enjoy her new career and to feel successful in using her talents.

In many situations this kind of conflict is not so clearly defined. Some women grow up with a vague feeling of discomfort whenever they do well in exams or succeed in their work. This may be because their family and friends do not really approve or reward that kind of success at all.

In some families approval is not given for personal achievement. It may be given for tangible evidence of other values such as serving the community or leading a very religious life or sacrificing oneself for others. Or approval may be reserved for merely being ordinary and mediocre and not outstanding in any way.

Or we may meet the situation where a girl is awarded the recognition but not the approval for her ability. A comment like this one does not induce a feeling of success: 'You've done well in science (or running or swimming or economics) this year, dear. You should have been a boy.'

Success can mean different things to us at different stages of our lives. But personal contentment may eventually depend on us recognising that we can enjoy our achievements and feel successful within ourselves even if we get little support from those close to us.

> EXERCISE
> **A list of achievements and opportunities**
> Now is the time to throw away any modesty, humility or reluctance you may have felt about your achievements. Start digging into your past and write down everything you have done that was recognised as an achievement by others. You might not have felt successful about it but others regarded it as an achievement. Maybe someone complimented you on your skills, work or a particular job you did. Maybe you were selected for a sporting team, the debating team or won an award for a painting you did. Write it down.
>
> Are you an excellent cook? A good hostess? A creative decorator of the house? Do you sew well? Are you a great mum? Write it down.
>
> One of the things we often do is brush off, gloss over or underestimate suggestions others make to us. Some of these may have been other people's recognition of our worth and ability which we were not able to accept as such at the time.
>
> Think back to whether anyone ever suggested you try for a competition, an award or a job. Did they suggest you ought to go on a committee or organise some project? Write down those suggestions even if you did not act on them.
>
> Now we are getting to the kind of thing meant by opportunities. People often point us in the direction of opportunities but we pass them by. Sometimes we are too nervous, afraid, insecure or modest to recognise we are being complimented on our ability and could do something about it.
>
> Next time anyone says: 'You know you should...',

WHAT IS THIS THING SUCCESS?

think about it. Maybe it is an opportunity that you should give some thought to following up.

This kind of list can help to resurrect lost self-esteem if you feel yours has been buried in the piles of nappies, baskets of washing, children's homework, husband's shirts or even your partner's interests and needs.

Keep it. It is a wonderful thing to look back on when things get tough.

5 GETTING THERE: VALUES AND GOALS

What are values?
Values are the ideas or beliefs which underlie many of the choices we make in our lives. They are the kind of things we often take for granted without understanding the influence they have on our patterns of behaviour.

In Chapter Four, I discussed briefly the influence our family's values can have on our view of the world and how we feel about being successful. In fact values extend far beyond our images of achievement to influence most of our views about life.

Usually we absorb values when we are children from our families, friends, schools and the general environment. Even as children we may have already encountered clashes in values between our friends and our own family or between school and other influences, and as a consequence, had to seek a compromise or make a choice about which course of action to follow.

Values are not made of stone
The common life crises at adolescence and mid-life occur because these are periods in our lives when our values are changing. There is a conflict between what we think we believe and what we need to believe and act on in order to feel comfortable with ourselves in our present and future lives.

Mid-life crises for women often start earlier than the traditional forties crises for men. From mid thirties to early forties is the common period in which women consciously or unconsciously re-examine their lives. Often this involves reassessing the values we have adopted earlier in life and choosing whether to reject some of them and/or give priorities to new values.

It can be very uncomfortable when we decide to adopt or acknowledge different values, emphasise new values or try to work out which values are more important to us at this stage of our lives. Sometimes it means leaving behind old friends or family who have chosen different paths. But it can also mean finding new friends and experiencing growth as people.

No-one works out the shift in values all at once, although we often have moments of insight or realisation along the way. Our assessment and shift in values may be a gradual change. When we find it difficult to adjust to the upheaval caused by these value shifts it is reassuring to realise others have done it before us. We are not the only ones to tread this path.

Conflict in values

Realising our values are different from others often explains why we feel uncomfortable with some individuals, argue with them or try to avoid them. Some people's driving motivations may be in direct conflict with the beliefs we hold to be most dear in life. Working or living with such individuals can be stressful unless we are able to compromise or agree to differ on basic issues. Holding opposite political viewpoints is a good example of an area where people face constant conflicts because of their differing values.

However, many of us have conflicts between some of our own values which need to be recognised and resolved. Acknowledging that we do have values which may seem in conflict with other values can help us to decide which ones we wish to give priorities to in particular situations.

EXERCISE
What are your dominant values?
The following list is a sample of the values women often believe in or accept as a basis to their behaviour.

It is important to realise no list of values could be comprehensive. Values are individual matters. Feel free to extend the list to suit yourself.

Read each value carefully and think about it before you tick whether it applies to you.
- Being independent – having the freedom to do things on my own.
- Using power – controlling the situation around me.
- Being a leader – influencing others, having followers.
- Being an expert in my field.
- Being fulfilled – realising my potential.
- Doing my duty – doing what is expected of me.
- Contributing to the welfare of others.
- Being liked by others.
- Meeting the family's needs.
- Looking after my own health – taking care of myself.
- Having companionship with others.
- Leading a balanced life.
- Feeling secure financially – not having to worry about present or future income.
- Feeling secure within myself – not worrying about what will happen to me in the future.
- Feeling pleasure in life – being happy and having fun.
- Being wealthy – earning a lot of money.
- Following a lifestyle based on religious beliefs.
- Being self-sufficient – supplying my own needs.
- Being creative – having the opportunities to use my creativity in my work.
- Gaining recognition for my own work.
- Achieving recognition for my contribution to the group.

- Being a rugged individual.
- Doing anything I do well.
- Leading an interesting life with varied experiences.
- Accepting my lot in life.
- Working to change society.
- Developing inner peace and harmony.
- Supporting a cause I believe in.
- Accepting people as they are.
- Standing up for what I believe in.
- Belonging to a group.
- Being neat and tidy.
- Leading a family-based life – centering my activities around my family's needs.
- Always learning.
- Gaining satisfaction from helping others to succeed.
- Being a devoted wife and mother.
- Being a help-mate to my partner.
- Enjoying nature in my hobbies and lifestyle.
- Believing strongly in health and fitness.

Having ticked the values which describe how you feel about life, now try to decide which of these are the most important to you. Write down the five or six most important and put them in order. Write today's date beside them.

Now reflect on the kind of life you wish to lead in three to five years and reconsider these values. Try to select the most important values for you in your future life. Write them down in the order you think will be most important to you in the future.

Finally, write down any conflicting values at present or in the future. What does that mean for you?

Now that you have thought about the values which are important for you both now and in the future you can use them as a framework to go to the next step of setting goals.

Unless you are clear on the views most important for you in your life, you will not be able to identify goals in harmony with your values. For example, if being a devoted wife and mother is a top value for you, your goals must take that into account. But your goals may be different if your top value is supporting a cause or being wealthy. Your recognition of your main values may mean choosing not to follow paths you thought you wanted.

Aims, objectives and goals

Often we decide we will aim to do things in our lives such as:
- getting fit and healthy
- spending more time with the children
- reading more
- doing a course
- getting a job
- relaxing more at weekends, and so on.

Or we might set objectives to:
- learn to fly an aeroplane
- write a book
- become a local councillor
- get a full-time job
- travel along the Amazon by boat, or whatever.

It is only when you ask yourself how you are going to do it all that you have to be specific. When we can work out specific aims and objectives we call them goals. Sometimes women find it difficult to work these out on the simplest level. They are too busy with day to day matters to be able to lift their heads and think about wider issues.

The next exercise is designed to help you clear your vision and think about aims and objectives you might set for yourself. After that you can set them as goals and then convert them to action plans.

EXERCISE
A future scenario

Find a time when you will not be interrupted to do this. Maybe you could go to a park, sit on a deserted beach or under a quiet tree in a forest or simply lie down on the floor of your living room and close your eyes when everyone is somewhere else for a couple of hours. Choose a place where you can relax and let your mind wander.

This is a time for putting aside practical restraints and allowing yourself to dream, to consider what you would like to do irrespective of any commitments you may have at the moment.

Now imagine what kind of person you want to be in, say, three to five years' time. Once you get used to doing this you can project yourself further, but start with a reasonable time frame. Take two years if that is as much as you can cope with at present. Now close your eyes and try to picture what kind of person you would like to be. Do not be frightened by what you are feeling. Do not reject it.

Cut yourself off from what you do at present and take a leap into the future – your future. Think about what you would be doing in your world there. Imagine your surroundings. Let your mind explore these for a while. You may be surprised how clearly you can imagine where you could be.

What kind of things would you be doing? What would be giving you satisfaction in your life? What would you really enjoy doing? Where should it be? Would it be home-based or in a different environment from where you are at present? What sort of home and family life would you enjoy in this situation? What country would you be in? What state? What surroundings? What kind of hobbies would you have? What lifestyle would you enjoy?

Now start writing down the kind of picture you

> have of your ideal scenario. Do not worry about how general it is to start with. Write it in notes, poetry, diagrams or drawings and symbols – anything which is meaningful and comfortable for you. Pick key words or ideas to start with especially if they express some of your values.

Sometimes when we allow ourselves to dream a bit we say things out of the blue which surprise us.

Yolanda was surprised when she began to explore her ideal future scenario. The dominating idea was that she wanted to have lots of money. Yet she realised that she had never admitted that to anyone else before.

Obviously this was suggesting a change of values for Yolanda which she would need to come to grips with before she could begin to work out how she could achieve her dream.

Because this is such an important process, I will describe in detail the way in which Jacinta has worked through the previous exercise over several years.

When Jacinta began to sort out her values and goals she had just started to look for part-time work and was feeling very depressed. She had completed a professional course while the children were young and was just beginning to consider her own needs now the children were going to school.

When Jacinta first started doing this kind of exercise she imagined herself in five years' time enjoying a mixture of creative work and responsibility. International recognition was one of the things which came into the picture of what she would be doing in her ideal world. She saw herself travelling overseas to speak at international conferences. She was also able to see herself quite clearly in a two-storied renovated terrace house which was very casually furnished.

As she went on in her imaginings Jacinta found that she had some good friends who shared her interest in work. She also had more time to spend with her husband to enjoy their relationship together in her ideal scenario.

Jacinta felt she was very self-confident in her ideal world in the future and could enjoy her children's company. She also incorporated her children into her working life and blurred the distinctions between family and work to enjoy both of them in a balanced way.

Out of this Jacinta started to make some very general notes of aims and objectives from the ideal scenario she had perceived.

Here are the notes she wrote down:
- being known and recognised in a field of endeavour
- building up networks of contacts in various fields
- building up lasting friendships through working with people on ideas, etc
- being creative in problem solving and writing
- living in an easy to look after house
- incorporating kids into our lives more
- having time with husband alone to enjoy our relationship
- some travel
- great self-confidence.

Jacinta realised that some of these fitted in with her current values while others emphasised different values. When she reviewed what her current values were she found that she had selected these as the six most important:
- being fulfilled
- being independent
- being an expert
- using power
- being a leader
- being wealthy.

However when she worked out what she would like her values to be in her ideal scenario they came out like this:
- being fulfilled
- being independent
- being an expert
- meeting my family's needs

- *looking after my health*
- *having companionship with others.*

Several years later Jacinta reviewed her progress. She has achieved considerable success in her career and personal life by working to meet her goals through developing an action plan (which we will look at later). She has experimented with various patterns of working and has eventually settled into a satisfying and creative role with a group of supportive, interactive people who share common values of combining family and work. Her depression has virtually disappeared.

When she considered her values again these came out to be the most important:
- *being fulfilled*
- *feeling secure within myself*
- *being creative*
- *developing inner peace and harmony*
- *meeting my family's needs*
- *leading an interesting life with varied experiences.*

In fact Jacinta's changes in dominant values have mirrored her needs through the process of adjusting to her new situation. However she could not have reached this point of satisfaction in life without working through how to achieve her targets in between.

Taking the journey is the adventure. Where we end up may not matter as long as it leads to developing inner peace and harmony and, like Jacinta, we can live the remainder of our lives feeling we have achieved some of our potential.

Categories for your goals

I have never actually broken down my own goal-setting into various categories. However you might find it more manageable to concentrate on some areas of your life for the moment and then look at other areas later on.

These are suggestions for areas you could select if you find it difficult to think of goals for yourself in a general sense:

- family life
- personal growth and development
- work and career
- enjoying life
- relationships with others
- financial aspects of life
- hobbies
- work developments
- a new job
- a different job
- spiritual development
- new opportunities
- political interests
- self-development
- skills development
- crafts
- family interests
- having more fun/enjoyment in your life
- family relationships
- fitness and health
- unpaid work.

Sometimes it is easier to set goals in a particular area of our lives, say, in terms of our family or our health, than in other broader areas where we have less control over what we can do. Later we can then review where we are going and decide whether we are now in a situation to change direction and pursue more long-term goals in, say, our work or relationships with others.

Putting goals into action

The most difficult stage in any change process is the action. It is very easy to talk about scenarios and plans and goals and write them down on paper. But if we are ever going to achieve goals we need to commit ourselves to doing something about them. This is where an action plan comes in.

Rather than let your future scenario present a list of goals which overwhelm you, let us work out which ones

are the most important for you. Then we can work backwards to a plan of action to make them happen. Let us look at some examples of this.
1 You decide on a very tangible goal of going off on a six month trip around Australia within three years. Now start working backwards as to what you need to be doing to achieve this. Some of these might be:
- become fitter
- save enough money to be able to take the time off without earning income for six months
- get used to camping out
- acquire bush skills
- learn how to change a tyre and do elementary maintenance on a vehicle.

This list then becomes the basis of your action plan for the next three years. Your action plan might take shape as follows:

You might decide to start your fitness program this week by running, jogging, exercising or going to a gym. On the money side, your first action may be to complete, within a month, a budget of how much you will need to save or earn in some way. Then your action plan will have to focus on a savings campaign (and here if you have a family you will have to have them on side) and/or some means of earning extra money through part-time work, lecturing, making goods for sale, and so on.

You might decide to test whether you (and anyone who is coming with you – a friend, your partner or your family) can tolerate camping. So to start with you might decide to borrow or hire some gear to go camping over a weekend. Or you might hire a van for a weekend.

To learn bush skills you might plan to do a course in the next six months. Your first set of actions could be to get information about who runs such courses, their cost, when they are, and so on.

On the issue of vehicle maintenance, you need to ferret out similar information on courses. Or you might tee up a friend to teach you personally every second weekend.

2. You decide to get yourself a job within two years when your youngest child will be at school. Start to work backwards on what you will need to do in order to make that possible. Your list might look like this:
   - decide on what type of job you would like to do
   - look at what training you might need to do to upgrade your skills
   - get the family organised to help with the housework
   - find friends or relatives or after-school care as support for looking after the children when necessary
   - talk to people who do this kind of work to find out more about it.

To decide what job you want you may start by reading the positions vacant columns in the local and daily papers. You could also decide to talk to friends and to employment agencies about opportunities in your area or district. Or you may have already picked a particular field as part of your values and goals.

You will need to set out what kind of things you want from the job. This might mean you decide to be assessed for your skills and interests by professional firms who offer that kind of service, in which case you might write down that the first action will be to find out who does this and how much they charge.

If your proposed job means extra skills you will need to take action in finding out where you can learn them, how much a course will cost, how often the courses are run, and the like. Your important action might be to book in to a course within six months.

Part of your action plan might be to discuss with the family which tasks they could do each day to gradually get used to helping more around the house.

Finally you can explore what you want to do with other people as part of your action. You might talk to day-care centres or your school to find out what they offer.

Time for your action

Now look at your own goals and decide which ones are most important for you to work towards immediately. An easy way is to put an A, B and C beside each one in order of importance. A shows the ones you care most about, B might be for the ones which you have less passion for and C might be trade-offs – things you would like but you can do without if the A's and B's come off.

Often when you begin to take action you realise the goals are inter-linking. Targets for one goal led to results in another, as in Rachel's case.

Rachel's goals included:
A to get more involved in a group of people
A to work to help the community
B to get involved in politics.

She realised that her action plan could combine all three if her target became: to find a political group which was friendly and interested in helping the community.

From there her action plan became:
1 To find out what political groups were in her area by the end of a fortnight.
   - ask her friends what they knew about local groups
   - read the local paper for any relevant information
   - check in the phone book for contacts
   - look at the notices in the local library.
2 To go to a meeting of a group within a month to see if it suited her.
3 To find other groups and go to meetings to see how they suited her in the following month if the first one was not of interest.
4 To join a group within six months.

In fact once Rachel started making enquiries she found that one of her friends was already a member of a political party and was happy to take her along to a meeting. She then found from talking to people at the meeting that there was a separate group working on the same community issues in which she was interested. Once she contacted that group she found an instant rapport with the people there and became an active member of the group and the political party. So Rachel was able to meet all three of those goals with one action plan.

Let us have another look at what Jacinta adopted as her goals based on her scenario. Firstly she worked out her preferences:

A   being known and recognised in a field of endeavour
A   building up networks of contacts in various fields
A   building up lasting friendships through working with people on ideas, etc
A   being creative in problem solving and writing
C   living in an easy to look after house
B   incorporating kids into our lives more
B   having time with husband alone to enjoy our relationship
B   some travel
A   great self-confidence.

Jacinta wrote down some goals from these preferences:
- to write articles and get them published
- to find a group of professional women who could provide both friendship and support in my career
- to join a professional group and develop more contacts professionally.

Following on this Jacinta began to make an action plan:
1 To sit down and write articles when they come into my head in order to get into practice at writing again. To start doing that this week.
2 To reserve a day a week (Tuesdays) for writing articles from this week onwards.
3 To write book reviews and get them published in a professional magazine within six months.
4 To start writing a book about a topic of interest.
5 To ring up tomorrow and get a membership form for the professional organisation I have been meaning to join for years.

6   To book in and go to a members' function in the next month.
7   To enquire today from people I know which organisation would help me in my profession.

What happened was that Jacinta did become more proficient at writing articles through sitting down and practising. Furthermore she enjoyed it enormously and found it satisfied her creative needs.

She forced herself to fill in the complicated form for membership of her professional organisation with some help from a friend. She then started to attend functions of interest and meet people who could be useful to her.

When she enquired about how to obtain certain book reviews published in the professional group's magazine she was told the editors were delighted to receive brief reviews particularly about books which were recent additions to their library. So Jacinta sent off several reviews and had them published. She did start writing a book which she went back to finishing three years later.

To follow up on a support organisation of women, Jacinta rang several friends and acquaintances for their opinions. One of them recommended that the only way to get anything out of an organisation was to work on a committee.

In fact Jacinta did not join the organisation of which her friend was part, but took her advice and joined another. Even though she did not know many people in the organisation she approached the president and said she was interested in being a committee member.

This was a valuable way of finding out how the group worked and meeting members of the group. It also gave her wonderful experience in developing her self-confidence and invaluable practice in working with groups – benefits which she later applied in her own business.

Six months later Jacinta reviewed her goals and realised she had already achieved most of them. She then reviewed her scenario and set new goals with an action plan to back them up. This included earning enough money to be able to support herself.

Her action plan included selling her professional services and publicising herself. By following up the contacts she had made through the two organisations she achieved this within a year.

Once she became established and confident in her business she also began to relax and work flexible hours to suit her family needs. This in turn fitted in with some of her other scenario requirements and began to reward her with the lifestyle she had envisaged.

Key points for action plans
The main points to remember about action plans are:
1 Break down each goal into as many action points as possible.
2 Make your first point seeking information.
3 Write down each specific action point in order to check later whether you did it.
4 Write down time frames and dates for both goals and action points. Make sure these are realistic – don't sabotage your chances of success by not allowing enough time for things to work out.
5 Follow up and achieve the tasks you set yourself.
6 Regularly review your action plans and goals. Be flexible enough to accommodate opportunities when they come your way.

Your action plan should be specific and realistic. Here is a pattern you might use as a model:

Target date	Action points
This week	gain information about...
This month	set aside time to...
By 30 August	discuss with my child/husband/boyfriend/parent...
Within a year	negotiate with my neighbour/child/boyfriend/friend/mother...
Within two years	form a group to...

By 1990   book in for...
discuss with my boss...
let my friends know I do not want to...
join a committee to...
go out on Mondays to...

How does all this fit in with seizing opportunities?

Some of you may feel puzzled at this stage because you believe that developing all that action planning cuts out rather than opens up the way for seizing opportunities when they come along. Only if you set your goals very narrowly will they limit you.

I have always defined my own goals fairly broadly. Then I have sought ways in which I could narrow them down to action plans relevant to my current situation and to meeting the opportunities which were within my sphere. In this way I have always found that the process of goal-setting has given me a fresh outlook on life. Knowing and recognising in what broad direction I would like to proceed seems to sharpen my awareness of how to react to the world around me. I have seldom found that it has had a narrowing effect.

In addition I have found that the action plan often leads me to opportunities which I did not realise existed or which were not relevant to me before. You will be amazed how your view of life changes once you have worked out your goals and action plans.

6 AFRAID OF BEING SUCCESSFUL?

Possible symptoms
Here are some questions for you to think about as an introduction to the idea of being afraid of success.
- Were you good at mathematics early in your school career but gave it up before you finished secondary school?
- Did you leave an unfinished course/diploma/degree in order to get married?
- Did you give up a promising career in order to get married and/or have children?
- Do you constantly choose to undertake tasks which are easily within your capacity so that you cannot fail to do them well?
- Do you often put off finishing something you have created because it will expose you to praise or recognition of your talent?
- When you are nearing the end of an ambitious project do you have a pattern of getting ill to the point where you decide you will give up and not finish it?
- When you are asked to give a talk or take on a task based on your experience do you find an excuse at the last moment to bow out?
- Do you regularly court failure by setting unrealistic goals for yourself and then willing the worst to happen?
- Do you insist on working for wages and still doing the house cleaning when you can afford to employ someone to do it for you?
- Will you end your life wishing you had achieved more with your talents than you are doing at present?

If you answered 'yes' to some of those questions it is possible you fall into the category of women who are suspected of 'being afraid of success'. Dolores seemed to fit into this category.

Dolores had wide experience in her family's well-known business. She was an active member of the board and had done well in academic courses which were partly developing her own interests and partly contributing to her expertise in the company.

When Dolores was asked to run an hour's session for a small group at a conference which was being organised especially for people working in her firm's industry she was pleased. This promised to be a breakthrough for her because even though her ability and contributions to the company at board meetings were highly regarded, some people felt she often undertook tasks which she never finished.

This time the conference was several months away and she had more than enough time to prepare her material. She sought people's advice about content and received a great deal of support and help from friends about what she could do to make the session more effective.

A couple of weeks before the conference she got cold feet and used her next study assignment as the excuse to bow out.

Maybe Dolores will finish some task she undertakes one day when she confronts whatever it is that hinders her from being able to succeed at anything.

This fear of succeeding as displayed by Dolores begins to explain why so many capable women do not volunteer for jobs or training which might stretch their capacity. Or when they do volunteer, as Dolores did, they never finish the task, they continually get cold feet.

The opportunities are so often there but we prefer not to take any risks. What if we fail? Better to stick with what we know than risk the challenge, excitement, frustration and possible humiliation of trying something which we might be able to do but which would not fit comfortably within our capacity. Or worse still, we could do the job but not perfectly.

Do you aim for perfection rather than success? Women often feel they have to complete tasks perfectly – even their housework. These compulsive perfectionists stop themselves from feeling satisfied and from succeeding in their lives.

Perfectionists are often people who strain compulsively towards impossible goals and measure their self-worth entirely in terms of their achievements. Because of this they are terrified by the prospect of failure. They face the dilemma of feeling driven and, at the same time, unrewarded by their accomplishments. Do you sometimes fit into this category? If so, you can do something about it.

More of the same or time for a change?

In Chapter Four I discussed the effects of conditioning on the way we feel about success. In the exercises in that chapter we concentrated on getting in touch with what had made us <u>feel</u> successful in our past, regardless of what we are <u>doing</u> at the moment. I believe this is invaluable in helping us to analyse which paths might suit us in the future. Getting in touch with those feelings of success can also be liberating. It brings with it the realisation that we can still feel successful in doing other things we might want to do <u>now</u>, even if in the past our families did not encourage us to follow these paths, or our values clashed with the people around us at school or in the neighbourhood.

We can change the direction of our lives at any age if we choose to, even though this seeking of new meaning is often associated with people in their late thirties and forties. At this point, many men as well as women begin to accept that life is finite and they begin to review their expectations and reach for unfulfilled potentials. They begin to pay attention to the needs of the other sides of their personalities, those sides which were neglected earlier. For women, this 'other' side is often epitomised by a desire for competence outside the home, for recognition and success.

We often associate 'mid-life crisis' with turmoil and discomfort, but it can be very fruitful once we have reassessed our values and tried to establish meaning for the remainder of our lives.

At school Alex had always been very successful in her studies because she was intelligent and did not need to work hard to do well. She never had to apply the discipline of real study. Her last few years of school were unhappy because of a move to a new school where she did not make friends.

She looked forward to going to university but once there the incentive and discipline to study hard still eluded her. This was partly because she needed to gain confidence and skills in other areas such as making friends and getting on with people after her disastrous experience at school. She never wanted to feel an outsider again so she did not spend much time studying. Her main efforts went into making firm friends and involving herself in student groups working on issues. She also joined the drama group which combined her interest in set and costume design with meeting people.

Because of her need to associate with people, she found, later in life, that her 'feeling successful' situations (see Chapter Four) all related to making friends. At university, on holidays and in work situations, her ability to get along with people had often been recognised and utilised.

However at 36, she felt she had talents she had largely ignored. She realised she needed to develop the creative side of her personality.

When she began a course in creative design she found that it was one of the most satisfying sensations she had ever experienced.

She also realised that to be any good at it she would have to apply herself in a way she had never learnt to do as a child. So she made some tough decisions. These included seeing her friends far less often and disciplining herself to spend long nights after her children were in bed and on weekends working on mastering techniques.

She gradually worked out a way of catching up with her friends that did not compromise her work. She was surprised how well she was able to stick to her tasks once she took her decisions seriously.

She went on to become proficient at design. Now she sees that it could lead her into a new career in a few years' time.

Research into the fear of success

Martina Horner is the person best known for her research in the USA on the issue of women being afraid of success.[1] In the late 1960s she established that some women became just as anxious when things went well for them as when they went badly. Many gifted women did not seem able to pursue success as men did. The more ability they had, the more anxious they became. Often this led to them losing the will to succeed. As a result they did not even finish courses in which they had demonstrated outstanding results.

According to Horner's studies the main reason for 65 per cent of the women she tested being disturbed at the prospect of success was the thought that doing well professionally would jeopardise their relationships with men. Either they would risk losing their boyfriends or never get them.

This contrasted strongly with 90 per cent of the men in the sample who were eager about the possibility of developing brilliant careers.

Colette Dowling discusses some of the aspects of this in her book, *The Cinderella Complex*.[2] The sub-title 'Women's Hidden Fear of Independence', sums up her results. She writes: 'It's not that women court failure; they avoid success... This tendency we have to scale ourselves down, to step back from our natural abilities rather than risk the loss of love, is a consequence of what I have referred to earlier as Gender Panic – the new confusion about our feminine identity. Rather than experience the anxiety of doing (and probably feeling unfeminine as a result), we don't do.'

Horner's study showed that the women who were not afraid of success tended to have less natural talent than those fearful of success, and that they were aiming for careers in rigorous scientific disciplines. Many of them came from working-class homes with mothers who were often better educated than their husbands and who had usually worked throughout their married lives. These women were likely to have aspirations that exceeded their actual ability – in theory. But they possessed the kind of push that got them much further in life than they might have done otherwise. I would suggest that <u>our chances of success in any field depend more on push, aspirations and hard work than on our measured ability by itself.</u>

After Leann finished school she did nursing training and then worked overseas in a variety of situations.

When she returned home she decided to study for a degree under a scheme specially developed to encourage adults wishing to return to university. However she was told that because she had not matriculated, she was not eligible. So she began to work out what she wanted to do with her life. She was very keen to progress in her nursing career so she started looking around for training opportunities and settled on a part-time course at a college of nursing which she completed very successfully. Her success was mainly due to her dedication and to the fact that she had warned her many friends in advance that she would be tied up for the year and unavailable for socialising. After her results came out she was able to see more of them.

In the meantime she was offered the chance to lecture in nursing in the institution where she had been working. This suited her very well and she found she enjoyed lecturing enormously. Nursing training became her new field.

Not content with this she found out what overseas scholarships were available and what courses she was interested in doing. Then the hard work began, filling in forms, going for interviews and coping with not being the winner. After several years of this she hit the jackpot. She won a scholarship to do 12 months' intensive study in a very respected institute in Europe.

When Leann returned from overseas she realised that she needed a university degree in education to give her a solid background in her chosen field.

When she enquired about doing an education course at the same university that had rejected her 10 years earlier Leann got a different reception. Her overseas study had included some subjects at a higher academic level than the undergraduate course covered. Not only was she now accepted into the university as an undergraduate but she was granted exemptions from some of the subjects.

Her results were excellent because she applied the same dedication to her studies that she had learnt earlier. When she graduated Leann had the satisfaction of being offered post-graduate studies.

Leann is a reminder of how much hard work and discipline is involved in achieving success.

She would probably appreciate the different view on this expressed by Joyce Nicholson when appointed to take over the family publishing business.

'You had better call me Managing Editor,' I said. 'I could not be Managing Director.'

My husband, a solicitor, was at the meeting ... 'Now' he said, 'Don't be bloody stupid. You have to be Managing Director. The Articles of the Association say so. Anyway, you know you can do it, if you set your mind to it.'

And so Joyce set her mind to it. She found out what many people do find out when they leap over the barrier to take risks and work at something at the limit of their experience:

'The other strange discovery was that when one occupies a certain position the knowledge I had feared I lacked automatically comes with that position ... For six months I did not raise my head from the desk. I did all the writing *and editing for three monthly journals and one annual reference book. The filing was in chaos. Important papers were missing. I worked practically every night and every weekend. But, as I had a part-time person at home to cook meals and do the housework, I enjoyed every moment of re-organising the business.'*[3]

In order to begin to enjoy your success and achieve some of your own goals you need to size up how much 'push' you will need, and whether you will be afraid to make it all happen.

Being aware of how you feel about success may help you decide how far you want to go and whether you need to confront how you have viewed it in the past.

Not being able to finish anything

Suzanne never seemed able to finish anything. Whenever given an important assignment as a graphic designer she would suddenly become ill. She missed deadlines and never achieved the success her talent promised. She craved mediocrity.

Through therapy Suzanne realised that her reasons for avoiding success could be traced to her childhood when her mother became successful in business. As a child she had felt very lonely when her mother worked long hours. She had also resented the relatives who had hung around when her mother became wealthy.

Once she realised these fears still had a powerful influence on her, Suzanne could begin to accept that she was far from mediocre and could begin to equate being successful with being happy and feeling good about herself. As a result her skills as a graphic designer began to be realised. She started meeting deadlines and enjoying the rewards that flow from success.

Sabotaging your partner

Some people who are in a marriage or relationship become trapped in the vicious circle of each partner sabotaging the success of the other. Often people who are unable to handle success unconsciously seek partners who feel the same way. They can then spend the rest of their lives putting the other one down and living in fear that their partner's successes will lead to their being loved less as a result.

Marita hid both herself and her talent as a painter behind dowdy clothes partly because she chose to remain a dabbler rather than a serious artist and partly because her husband, John, encouraged her to remain unattractive and unknown.

On the other hand John worked in a sophisticated city office and revelled in always being immaculately dressed in expensive clothes. When either of them attempted to discuss successes they had achieved in their respective jobs the other deprecated the achievement. This often led to each one feeling let down instead of being elated about the success of the day.

Through therapy Marita realised that she was terrified of success because as a child she had equated losing her friends and ruining her life with the move her family had made to a wealthy neighbourhood.

Once she came to grips with these fears she was able to change her attitude and begin to enjoy her talents. She started to dress herself in far more interesting clothes and looked forward to feeling much more successful as an artist than she had dared to in the past. A gallery was keen to display her paintings and she met the challenge.

What can you do about confronting 'fear of success'?

Whether you associate with any of the examples I have given depends entirely on your personal experiences.

Many of us are brought up to put each other down. We often cut down 'tall poppies'. Our relatives and friends may put us down as effectively as do our partners. Recognising that we can do something about it is a good place to start. Then we can plan to attack the destructive process.

One constructive way of managing this is to bring out into the open the issue of mutual put-down. You can do this with friends, relatives or family, provided there is mutual trust.

One approach is to list and discuss actual examples of where 'putting down' has occurred. You can then use these as a basis for starting to build each other up. Allow the other person to enjoy the feelings of success that come from little things that happen in the day. You can then rejoice in the satisfaction of sharing your warm feelings of success with the people who are closest to you.

Mutual encouragement is very rewarding in building each other's self-esteem and happiness.

Success and failure versus not trying at all

Fear of success particularly for women has also been linked with a fear of failure. If you have a go at something you might fail at it and feel terrible. If you do not risk trying something then you cannot be hurt if you fail.

Many of us have not learnt how to build up defences against the negative feelings which failure can arouse. So we settle for a bland emotional life and seek to avoid both success and failure and any of the risks, apprehension and excitement they might bring. This can easily lead to boredom.

One of the ways of coping with a fear of failure is to live and appreciate each day at a time rather than allowing yourself to live too much in the future. This enables you gradually to realise that the excitement of actually going for an important interview or of being recommended for a position is something you can enjoy in itself for the moment. It is an experience in its own right whether it leads on further or not. It is also part of increasing your experience and personal learning.

This does not mean that, at the same time, you do not hope to get the position. You admit that you would love to get there – and you acknowledge that you will be disappointed if you do not make it, but you will cope with that emotion too and not be devastated by it. You must not reject the possible elation of success just because you might also feel the cold winds of failures.

Building on a loss to see an opportunity

A couple of years ago I applied for and was interviewed for several jobs within two months of each other. I wanted both of the jobs at the time and I was particularly disappointed for a day or two after I heard that I had not got either one.

In both cases I rang up to enquire why I had not been selected. I then started to digest the information I was given, which was very valuable for me. Losing the second job was a turning-point.

I realised that the abilities and skills I had were insufficient and perhaps not even relevant to the jobs I had been considered for. In the light of this I reassessed whether I was prepared to do further study in order to aspire to similar positions later on – or whether I needed to follow other paths.

I decided that studying did not appeal to me then – I would prefer to gain more experience by working in my own business; and it was time to start developing some ideas I had already talked about to other people.

I had hoped I would succeed in those jobs and when I did not I certainly felt disappointed, but I did not feel a failure. In fact I was able to build on the disappointment to go on to a more interesting and satisfying career than either job could have given me. I had to seriously reconsider my goals. For me this involved setting more realistic ones.

Often we do not succeed at things because we set unrealistic goals. It is important not to set ourselves goals which have failure already built into them. Reconsider your goals if necessary and aim for ones which will be attainable and which will reward you with those warm feelings about yourself.

Part of living with success is being able to acknowledge

AFRAID OF BEING SUCCESSFUL?

the bitterness of disappointment and then being able to pick yourself up to reassess what your goals are: whether you want to revise them to make them more realistic and attainable or whether you need a new action plan to reach those goals via a more circuitous route.

Try to enlist the support of family and friends along your path to success. It will be much more satisfying if together you appreciate the sweetness of success and together you cope with the bitterness of failure.

EXERCISE
What were your answers?
Seriously consider the questions at the beginning of this chapter. Write 'Yes' or 'No' beside them.

If you answer 'Yes' to some of these questions, have the ideas discussed in this chapter meant anything to you?

Write down one action you will take to begin to confront how you feel about being successful in the future.

EXERCISE
Will success change you?
Try to imagine you are successful in some of the dreams you have set yourself. How do you feel about it?

Write down some of the things you realise might change in your life. These could include:
- your relationship with your husband or partner
- time available to spend with your children
- time available to spend with your parents and close relatives
- how your relatives regard you
- time to spend with your present friends
- how your friends regard you.

How do you think these changes could affect you and your attitude to feeling successful?

7 A CAREER ON YOUR OWN TERMS

Over the years I have read many books designed to assist women to develop their careers and ambitions. Some have been excellent, but I have always felt they lacked something. The variety of success experiences people achieve in their lives are not restricted to climbing pyramids in the work place. Many of life's meaningful work experiences happen beyond big offices.

One view of the pyramid

The main emphasis of many books is the company career, getting near the top of a small or large pyramid in an organisation. They suggest strategies which are not simple to achieve with a family and fail to satisfy many women's needs and values.

Once I employed a full-time housekeeper who was very competent to look after my children then aged four and eight. I forsook my home office looking out on the garden to work in a multi-storied city building with a magnificent view of the city, especially its sunsets. This became one of the traps of the position.

Who wants to catch glimpses of sunsets from a tall city building day-in day-out while your children are having their dinner and your meal is keeping warm till you arrive home too tired to enjoy it and definitely too tired to pay adequate attention to your children before they go to bed? I soon came to the conclusion that I did not.

I was so tired at weekends that my priority became to sleep like a zombie to face the next week rather than to enjoy the company of my children or tolerate their noisy friends.

I gradually realised after about six months that this kind

of life was not satisfying my own needs or values or my family's welfare. And it was not going to improve.

I began to work through the sort of process I've outlined in Chapter Five, leading me to apply for jobs which could give me the flexibility to spend time with the children and develop my own ideas as well.

When I was not offered these jobs I decided to take the plunge, resign anyway and start working for myself in a field I had been interested in for some time. I have not looked back since.

Later, I began to appreciate the vast experience I had gained from the zig-zag path my career had taken. I also saw it as a great strength that I had not been trapped in a 'pyramid-climbing' exercise and I could resign and try other avenues with the confidence that the big organisation was not the only way to go. What do I mean by a zig-zag path in a career? Let me quote Virginia Cuppaidge, a successful artist.[1]

'There's no road map. It's only in retrospect that you can plot the course of your life, looking backwards from the point where you find yourself to the point where you began. My paintings are very much about the phenomenon of dealing with life on the magic level, re-inventing it as you go along. I did a painting recently that I think sums up my life both personally and artistically. It's called "The Road Less Travelled". '

I suggest to you that many of us can develop lives which will be aptly recognised as 'Roads Less Travelled' but which can give us alternatives to the pyramid path for achieving success and fulfillment on our own terms.

And for many women the path less travelled will take the form of a zig-zag which allows you to detour to try other things and go back later to your original job or career or study if that is what you want. It may also mean that the detours become a way of life in themselves.

The zig-zag path could include part-time work, being self-employed, negotiating flexible hours, or becoming interested in study, politics, music, art or writing. It could embrace taking the children overseas or around Australia as a great detour in your career which could lead you to other interests or give you invaluable insights in your next job. Above all, it encourages you to explore alternatives to satisfy your career needs and your values within your particular situation.

The participants in a 'Career Planning For Women' course I ran worked out an excellent definition for 'career' as a basis for the course. They agreed that a 'career' meant 'combining meaningful work with personal life to accommodate personal growth and dynamism'. I like this definition. It fits in very well with the spirit of the zig-zag path which can offer infinitely more possibilities for women to follow to give us flexibility in living and open up our choices.

Crises, crucibles and careers

Recently I reviewed the marital status of the members of a professional women's group committee with which I had been involved. I realised I was the only woman still married to her first husband and looking after children.

This came as a bit of a shock to me. It also made me realise why I found it difficult to discuss my career-versus-family concerns with those friends. They could scarcely understand my concerns since theirs were so different. I realised these women were representative of career women in Australia in the early 1980s.

Over the years I have followed with interest the career stories of a number of notable women in Australia. With exceptions, very few have had the combination of ongoing marriages, raising children and managing their high-flying career paths.

Often it has been the need to cope with being widowed, separated or divorced which has served as a crucible for these women to make their way independently in the world and achieve success and rewards which may not have come their way.

They are perhaps more remarkable for having brought up and provided for their children alone while pursuing demanding careers.

I began to wonder whether many women once they are settled with responsibilities for looking after other people or maintaining relationships need similar crucible-like experiences to push them to explore other alternatives – to grasp their lives with both hands and develop their latent abilities.

The experience may not be as severe as losing your husband or being divorced. It may simply take the form of a personal review of your life and what you are getting out of it because you feel you are depressed with nowhere to go. Or it may be a chance remark, an opportune poster or an experience of injustice or righteous indignation as a parent, rate-payer or tax-payer which inspires you to rouse yourself to fight for a social cause or nominate for the school or local council, go into politics or develop new organisations.

Politics at all levels presents ideal choices for any woman to consider as the next stage of a zig-zag career path. You do not have to study at college or university to represent your neighbours on a council or a government. Experience, hard work and strategies will help you much more as the following examples of successful politicians demonstrate.

Joan Child definitely travelled the zig-zag path to her position as the Speaker in the House of Representatives, the lower house of Federal Parliament in Australia.

Joan has had more than her share of trials to deal with in her life. Widowed in 1963 and left with five sons to raise when she was in her early thirties, Joan found her widow's pension inadequate for her family.

An account of her early life emphasises her indignation at the attitudes expressed towards her as a widow when she was interviewed for her pension.[2] *Further experience as a factory hand taught her a lot more about injustice, especially concerning the migrant women she met there.*

Spurred by her experiences, Joan became very involved in the Australian Labor Party. This led to her becoming Branch Secretary and State Delegate and working on campaigns.

In between she worked in a dress shop and then doing housework for others which gave her the flexible hours needed to care for her children. Joan did housework in 1972 to earn the money she needed for her own campaign.

When she lost the seat by only 308 votes in 1972, Joan says that it was probably the best thing to happen as she realised she simply was not experienced enough at that stage to go into Federal Parliament.

The day after the election a campaign meeting laid plans to win the seat, which she did in 1974. By then Joan's children had all left school, making it easier for her to do the job.

When Joan was defeated on the fateful 13 December 1975 election, she planned, before she went to bed that night, to win back the seat. She did this once more after her 1977 defeat before finally winning the seat in 1980.

Since then Joan has taken a high profile, representing Australia first as a parliamentary delegate to Scandinavia and then as the elected delegate to the European Council and European Parliament. Back at home she became Deputy Chairwoman of Committees, then Chairwoman before taking on her role as Speaker.

Another woman who took up politics to fight for her social beliefs is Jo Vallentine. Jo was brought up on a farm and became interested in nuclear disarmament when in the United States as an exchange student. And later as a mother she became a peace activist.

The backing of the Nuclear Disarmament Party and her own personal commitment to the cause led to her victory as the world's first elected peace party politician in 1984.

She is another example of someone choosing a career on her own terms. She gave up her first paid job in 12 years to run for the Senate, to fight for what she believes is the most important issue of all.

She is determined to keep her Quaker integrity in her role as a Senator and felt one of the hardest tasks in her new career would be leaving her three- and five-year-old daughters and her husband when her Senate term began.

In keeping with her beliefs she had no plans to move into the traditional politician's city office once her Senate allowances were paid. She hoped instead to find an old house on the edge of Perth where her supporters could easily find a park and feel at home when they brought their children along.

Local politics are attracting increasing numbers of women. Getting elected to the local council or shire can be an excellent step to renewing your self-confidence and going on to other jobs. Alternatively, some of the women get so involved in the business of local government that they work to have more control. Recently, a quarter of Melbourne's local councils had women mayors.

On the local government council front the election of Sallyanne Atkinson, mother of five, as Brisbane's and Australia's first woman Lord Mayor in 1985 illustrates another case of a woman developing a career through her interest in politics.

What are social entrepreneurs?

Personal experiences have often led people to become what I call 'social entrepreneurs'. Women often take these paths through personal experiences or convictions – some crucible-like situation brings them to the point where they take action to back up what they believe.

These situations may lead them to start a simple self-help organisation for people sharing a common situation which may eventually grow further and spread to a national or international level. Or they may devote their energy to personally promoting a cause such as nuclear disarmament or breast feeding babies or some other cause which they are prepared to fight for in order to have it recognised by society.

The energy, drive and single-mindedness which they devote to these causes is similar to the qualities which drive other men and women in the commercial sphere to set up businesses, produce publications, or fill a gap in the market with a superior service.

Here are several examples of women who, as 'social entrepreneurs', have founded successful organisations.

Kaaren Fitzgerald founded the Sudden Infant Death Research Foundation (SIDRF) after the tragic loss of one of her children. Sudden Infant Death is commonly called 'Cot Death' and is recognised as a world-wide problem.

Kaaren is now the President and Executive Director of SIDRF. After founding the organisation in 1977 she worked long hours getting the foundation funded and recognised.

SIDRF employs 16 people, handled a budget for 1984–85 of $250 000 (which excludes the promotions' unit for fundraising) and mails out a regular newsletter to about 4000 interested people.

When talking to Kaaren I was struck by her enthusiasm for all of her jobs. I was also impressed by the fact that she has a vision of how she is growing as a person and of what the organisation will be able to achieve. She has a time-line on her wall of where SIDRF will be in 1988 and what steps are needed in order to achieve the projected growth and development.

She also admits, like so many entrepreneurs, that had she known seven years ago what she was embarking on she would never have had the courage to start. She also recognises that deciding to develop a fund has opened up opportunities for her own personal growth that she would never have imagined possible.

In addition to her ongoing responsibility for SIDRF, Kaaren is actively involved in a family business, run from a home office. She also looks after her home and four children and finds time to follow another interest, being a marriage celebrant.

When she thinks about her philosophy in developing

SIDRF Kaaren believes it is best summed up as 'giving individuals the opportunity to grow'. This happens to the people who use the organisation when they are seeking some way of coping with their own grief following the loss of a child. It also happens to those who decide to stay involved in SIDRF to support the cause. Some of these parents decide to do training themselves and become volunteer home visitors for the group. Kaaren sees that she can offer women who may have spent most of their time at home the chance to take on new roles and develop their talents in working with the organisation.

Kaaren is an example of a 'social entrepreneur' who draws on her abilities to build and drive an organisation which she is convinced needs to be in place to plug some of the gaps in our society. I believe that this kind of role is one that many women choose as an unpaid career, sometimes in smaller organisations, other times in large charity groups, where they often find ways of satisfying their social or creative needs as well as contributing to society on their own terms.

The Nursing Mothers' Association of Australia (NMAA) represents an outstanding example of women's acumen in voluntarily founding and running an organisation to support a cause in which they believe very strongly.

It was founded by Mary Paton and five other mothers in 1964. Mary had the idea of selling products related to their members' needs to keep the membership fees low. The success of this innovative strategy is easily demonstrated by the fact that 20 years later, the annual membership fee was still only $10 per person.

Their first product was the 'Meh Tai' which proved very useful for carrying young babies around while leaving mothers' hands free to do other tasks. Since then they have financed their organisation through publishing and marketing other products such as lambskins, plastic 'puddle suits', cookbooks and educational material.

They have a board of 12 directors, a system of local

branches and an invaluable network of counsellors who are trained and available to help mothers individually with problems of breast-feeding.

Members of the NMAA have encouraged people to open similar organisations in a number of other countries. Their turnover is more than a million dollars annually and more than 75 000 people have joined as members.

The NMAA is an excellent example of how successful women can be as social entrepreneurs.

Recognising the 'not-for-profit executive'

The final list of 12 outstanding executives out of the 100 or more nominations *Savvy*, the American magazine, received in 1985 for its community projects roster demonstrates the wide variety of organisations women are involved in as managers and social entrepreneurs.

The final roster featured executives of the Girl Scouts, Family Services, the Planned Parenthood Federation, United Way (an organisation to assist Spanish-speaking people in their community), a school district, the National League for Nursing, Goodwill Industries of Arkansas (which places handicapped people in jobs), a run-down YMCA branch and the Children's Television Workshop (of Sesame Street fame).

One of the most encouraging things about these women was that many of them had few commercial qualifications to bring to their present positions – a reminder that it is often ability and drive rather than training and experience that enables women to achieve success.

Going creative

As part of developing careers on their own terms, women have often used their skills in crafts or arts or design or writing to give them a flexible lifestyle. This may be for personal fulfilment and development rather than as a means of earning money.

Often women who start some form of creative activity

as an interest end up finding themselves in a different career niche. Whether they find it more frustrating to limit their creative output to fit in with family demands than women in more orthodox job situations can only be speculated.

Marea Gazzard's career shows a zig-zag path from working as a legal secretary, to doing ceramics for interest, to doing full-time study in the craft both in Australia and overseas, to holding successful exhibitions. As a wife and mother, this potter with a world-wide reputation, gives us some insights into the life she leads.[3]

'There's nothing romantic about it. I start at eight and finish at three. I'd like to be able to wake up and go straight to work, but you can't do that. There's the family to think of. I do a lot of sketches. When you get into a working rhythm, good things might happen. You might get obsessed with an idea that lasts two years in your mind before you turn it into something physical. It's an image. A line. A movement you see in something. I work in coils because it's freer but I think the basic reason I became so involved with coils is far less artistic. I found I could cover up my work and come back to it later. Which was very useful with children!'

Some women have become notable in the film industry in recent years. Women like Pat Lovell have expressed their creative drive by working extremely hard to achieve their ends.

Pat was in her early forties when she decided to make the now internationally recognised film, Picnic at Hanging Rock. *She had been an unfulfilled film-maker since her school days. She said that vocational guidance people shook their heads and said that it was impossible because she was a girl.*

She says that producing her first film was 'the most intensely creative thing I've done apart from having the kids'.[4] *It took from 1971, when she first read the book,* Picnic at Hanging Rock, *till 1975 before she started making the film.*

She is an inspiring example of a woman determined to succeed. She could have given in many times along the way with the obstacles she encountered.

Both films and theatre can offer a wide range of roles for women. They may choose to be playwrights, actresses, designers, directors, producers or get involved in the running and administration of a theatre or production. Some of these people expressed their views on their work in an interesting article, 'The Script, a Bigger Role for Women'.[5]

Progress, promotions and the zig-zag

Increasingly it is acknowledged that people need to gain experience in a variety of organisations even for a steady career development.

Nowadays it is much more likely that changing from one firm to another, moving about from one city to another or even from one country to another may open up more opportunities for experience and advancement than staying in the same organisation for ever.

Several years ago I heard a talk about opportunities on how journalists could progress in their careers. The point was made that women journalists often got stuck in the low levels of a 'good' newspaper. It is difficult for these women to progress in their careers unless they are prepared to get out of their comfortable niches and gain broader experience working in less prestigious country or suburban papers.

It would seem that the zig-zag path may even be necessary for people like journalists.

Some examples of the zig-zag path
Many women choose a path along these lines. It enables them to take up part-time work and then full-time work as their children grow up.

A CAREER ON YOUR OWN TERMS

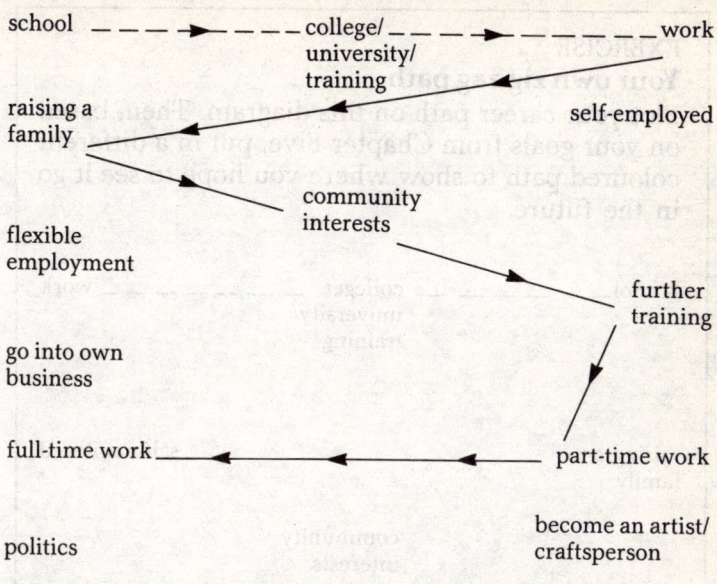

My own career so far has followed this path:

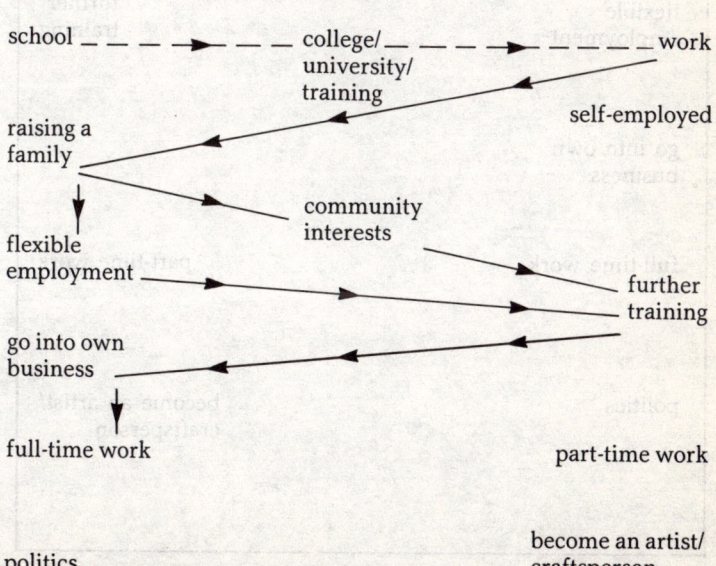

EXERCISE
Your own zig-zag path

Plot your career path on this diagram. Then, based on your goals from Chapter Five, put in a different coloured path to show where you hope to see it go in the future.

school _ _ _ _ _ _   college/ _ _ _ _ _ _ _ work
                      university/
                      training

raising a   self-employed
family

              community
              interests

flexible   further
employment   training

go into own
business

full-time work   part-time work

politics   become an artist/
                                       craftsperson

Here are some examples of career options you might consider if you want to pursue a career on your own terms:
- Becoming a counsellor for a self-help group like Nursing Mothers' Association or Sudden Infant Death Research Foundation.
- Running courses in areas in which you have expertise, either voluntarily or for money.
- Helping to set up or run a local community house.
- Supporting a local group which supports a cause you believe in.
- Working to set up a community facility of any kind.
- Starting up a local group to discuss issues or ideas of particular interest to you.
- Running a church group you are interested in.
- Nominating yourself for the school council.
- Running as a candidate for the local council or shire.
- Getting elected to local council and/or becoming a mayor.
- Seeking part-time teaching or lecturing in topics in which you have had experience.
- Running part-time services from home.
- Developing and running your own courses commercially.
- Joining a political party and seeking a position on a committee working on issues of interest to you.
- Joining a political party and getting elected to a seat in parliament.
- Developing art or craft products and selling them at weekend markets or through a shop on commission.
- Teaching craft classes.
- Developing a skill you can sell as a course or as a consultant.
- Moving out of school teaching into lecturing or other avenues after retraining.
- Moving into a managerial position in a school as a headmistress.
- Becoming an artist, author, poet, playwright, painter, sculptor or whatever, to develop your creative talents.
- Retraining to become a technician, electronics' engineer,

plumber, car mechanic, carpenter or whatever you desire.
- Retraining to become a lawyer, scientist, economist, teacher, nurse, manager or whatever you wish.
- Becoming a departmental head in your institution.
- Running your institution as the director.
- Using retraining in any field to get into tertiary institutions and then into other opportunities.
- Becoming well-known and respected in a field of work you enjoy. You then let people know that you are interested in work and people approach you to join them or do something because they need your experience.

Finally, remember our definition of 'Career': 'Combining meaningful work with personal life to accommodate personal growth and dynamism'.

8 THE NEW YOU: LIVING WITH IT

If you are feeling ambivalent about the changes you are making in your life this is a good time to reconsider where you are coming from and how much you can cope with before you go on to the next stage of growth.

Here are some reflections which have meant a lot to me over the years. Often I have read them for reassurance in times of doubt, tiredness and ambivalence.

First, a gem from the Talmud: 'If I am not for myself, who will be for me? If I am for myself only, what am I? If not now – when?'

Secondly from Alice Sargent, author of *Beyond Sex Roles*.[1]

'I am constantly engaged in my own struggle to achieve greater self-actualization, rather than submitting or succumbing to living for and through others. Many times I have been tempted to abandon my total self to a lesser sense of self, thereby letting the noise of life drown me. After all, I am just a woman with work, teaching and groups, husband, a child, friends, and parents. Many times I wish I had someone to prepare dinner, play with our child, plan my social life, and soothe my confused ego. Many times I give in and find myself living to work and problem-solve as many people do, rather than working and problem-solving to live. Many times, I lose my focus and start living for others to the exclusion of myself; then I scan those around me for their expectations rather than charting my own course. I start fulfilling my sex-role proscriptions of being deferential; smiling a lot; not being too assertive with men or confronting with women; looking for confirmation of my work competency and femininity from men, and affirmation of my competence as a mother and homemaker from women. After that, for a brief space, I become refocused and feel a solid balance between my concern for others, my interest in work, my sense of my own competence, my direction, and my sense of fun and joy in my life. I feel like a sailboat that is righted after having been inundated by a strong wind, and I let go for a while until the next gust.'

So if you are feeling buffeted by the winds of change you can be reassured that others have felt that same buffeting and have come through.

The chaos and confusion of change

Never underestimate the effect of change on people's lives. When you are introducing anything new into an organisation (I include the family as one) you need to allow for emotional responses to it. I believe people can cope with change and enjoy the improvements provided there is adequate planning, and allowances are made for the period of adjustment.

People often do not like change because:
- they are afraid of the new and unfamiliar
- they enjoy the established and known rituals of life and find them reassuring
- they do not see how a change can benefit them.

When I run 'Personal Career Development' courses, I try to run them over two or three weeks with sessions one week apart to allow people time to work out what they are feeling about the changes they are making to their lives.

Course participants often tell me in the second session that they are feeling very puzzled and uncertain. Sometimes they recognise feelings of anger as a reaction to their lost dreams or loss of control. Other times they want to know why they have not felt successful or are concerned about their changing values.

Often the only way people are able to change is to work

through this painful, confusing process of sorting out and acknowledging the past, coming to grips with it and then moving on to the future with new convictions and hopes. After all, this is what taking control of your life is all about. Eventually it can be exhilarating!

This process of adjusting to change may be more intense for people who take quite radical steps into new career paths where they have to learn new skills very quickly. They are often surprised afterwards about how exhausting this process can be.

Many of us assumed that when we sorted out our painful teenage years we had finished with that kind of thing. Of course this is seldom the case. Being a teenager is only one of the developmental periods in a person's life. People in their thirties and forties often liken their mid-life evaluation to how they felt as teenagers and find it just as painful.

If we realise this happens to other people as well as to ourselves we do not have to feel so confused and need not be afraid of admitting it. We can be reassured that we should keep on with the process of change, knowing that even if the sides are rocky at times there really is a light at the end of the tunnel.

Making some space for yourself

If you are feeling very affected by the changes you are making, you may need to carve out a bit more space either temporarily or permanently, for relaxing and thinking. Mothers may find this particularly difficult to do. But I suggest that it will help you in the long run.

What do I mean by making some space for yourself? Try taking off a couple of hours away from the house at night or at weekends when your husband, partner or friend can look after the children. Sit down quietly with a cup of tea or coffee in pleasant surroundings. Look around a gallery. Drive up into the country. Chat to a friend by yourself. Even shopping by yourself and taking the chance to browse can be relaxing.

THE NEW YOU

Flying the coop

'If things get too bad altogether you may have to "fly the coop" for a couple of days and leave the family to cope by themselves. You'll be amazed how many other women have done it. While you're away you'll have time to calm down and look at things in their proper perspective. It's possible you have been trying to do too much and not getting enough rest. Your family will have time to realise that your complaints were serious and that something has to be done. Don't be too proud to talk things over with friends and relatives. Better to use these escape routes when you need them than to become hooked on Valium or keep pushing yourself until you have a nervous breakdown.'[2]

One desperate Saturday lunchtime a few years ago, I really needed to get away for a while and simply told my husband that I was going away for a couple of hours. I ended up going to the only place where I could get a reasonable cup of coffee and sit down and think on a Saturday afternoon – the local indoor bowling complex. Later I drove back and parked outside my next door neighbour's house.

My neighbours were surprised and intrigued when I explained I had parked my car outside because I had run away. They were also sympathetic and supportive.

After discussing some issues with them I went home more able to face the family. I have met friends since who have done similar things at odd times.

I have also taken myself off for a holiday for a couple of days when I realised I needed a complete break to pick up physically and/or mentally.

You can find quite practical and even creative solutions to having someone else look after your children when you decide to take a weekend off to be alone or with your partner or friend or whatever. Try it. You will not be the first one to carve out a bit more space for yourself. And you will feel much better for it.

Rest and your health

Perhaps you have not had enough rest if things are beginning to get you down. At times when I feel I am getting worn down by the cares of the family and the world I take myself to bed early (8.30 pm to 10 pm is early for me) and have a good night's sleep. Somehow things appear less disastrous in the morning! Try at least one night a week to be in bed by 9.30 pm.

I am much better at taking rest these days than I used to be. I learnt my lesson about health the hard way. Soon after starting my own business I developed glandular fever. This was partly due to the stress of trying to meet strict deadlines. I really pushed myself some nights to prepare proposals – and I kept wondering why I felt so exhausted.

I now believe that falling ill was a blessing in disguise. It has helped me to be much more aware of relaxing when I am under stress and has possibly saved me from suffering burnout (which we look at later on in this chapter).

I recovered well by obeying the doctor's instructions about rest. Even though I missed out on one assignment at the time, I did get the chance to do work on the second stage of that project later.

The lesson I learnt was that my health was very important, it was the key to my being able to work at all! I realised that I had to obey the signals my body was giving me. As a result, I now rest more often than I ever did before I was ill – and I feel more alive for it.

If I am exhausted from working to a deadline or have just finished a big assignment I allow myself to take time off. This might mean enjoying a few hours' shopping, going for a walk, a swim or a sauna or merely sitting in the sun for a while. I have also learnt the value of a 'cat nap'.

Rest before you get stressed

We all need a bit of stress to give us some of the excitement and satisfactions of life. If we all led very bland lives which never involved any tension at all we would be bored. However there is a need to balance our tension levels.

Stress management involves recognising when we are under stress, what our particular symptoms are, and how we can adopt new patterns of behaviour to cope with these symptoms so that our lives are not seriously disarrayed.

Excessive stress

There are some general signs which indicate excessive stress. The following are signs which should prompt you to go to a doctor straight away to have a check-up: chest pain, palpitations, undue shortness of breath, indigestion, migraine or tension headaches, muscle tension – shoulders/back of neck, inability to concentrate, lethargy/low level of energy, increased irritability, poor sleep, excessive perspiration, skin rashes, muscle tremors, sexual difficulties.

> EXERCISE
> **Life events as sources of stress**
> The following list has been developed by Drs Thomas H Holmes and Richard H Rahe, psychiatrists at the University of Washington Medical School, based on incidents which can increase stress levels. If some of these incidents occur together you can be under very high stress levels, often through no fault of your own. And you certainly need to be aware of the possible danger to your health as a result of such high and often unexpected tension[3].
>
> According to the researchers of this stress scale, a person's yearly stress accumulation can be used as a guide to the likelihood of that person becoming physically or emotionally ill during the following two years.
>
> If you have a score of less than 150 for the past year you have only a 37 per cent chance of becoming

ill in the next two years. If your score is between 150 and 300 your chances of an illness in the next two years increase to 51 per cent. But if your score is more than 300 your chances of having a serious illness within two years increase to 80 per cent.

The stress of adjusting to change

Events	Scale of impact
Death of spouse	100
Divorce	73
Marital separation	65
Jail term	63
Death of close family member	63
Personal injury or illness	53
Marriage	50
Fired from work	47
Marital reconciliation	45
Retirement	45
Change in family member's health	44
Pregnancy	40
Sex difficulties	39
Addition to family	39
Business readjustment	39
Change in financial status	38
Death of close friend	37
Change to different line of work	36
Change in number of arguments with spouse	35
Mortgage or loan for major purchase (home)	31
Foreclosure of mortgage or loan	30
Change in work responsibilities	29
Son or daughter leaving home	29
Trouble with in-laws	29
Outstanding personal achievement	28
Spouse begins or stops work	26
Starting or finishing school	26
Change in living conditions	25
Revision of personal habits	24

Trouble with boss	23
Change in work hours, conditions	20
Change in residence	20
Change in schools	20
Change in recreational habits	19
Change in church activities	19
Change in social activities	18
Mortgage or loan for minor purchase (TV)	17
Change in sleeping habits	16
Change in number of family gatherings	15
Change in eating habits	15
Vacation	13
Christmas season	12
Minor violation of the law	11

Tick any of those which have occurred to you over the past year. Now add up the total impact score you have accumulated over the year. How does it compare with the research findings on your chances of a serious illness in the next two years? If your chances appear high you should be aware of your need to find ways of coping with the stress in your life and take actions to increase the care you take of your own health.

EXERCISE
Stress events in your recent life
This is a list of more specific events which can cause stress as part of our changing lives. I have separated them into ones which directly affect you and others which, by happening to those close to you, also affect your life. What scale of impact would you give to these specific events on your stress levels compared to Holmes and Rahe's scale?
Events affecting you directly
Death of a child
Death of a parent
Death of a close friend

Facing a court case
Becoming handicapped or deformed
Being seriously ill
Being involved in a car accident
Discovering an unwanted pregnancy
Moving to live in a new country
Losing a job
Breaking up a close relationship
Starting a new job
Starting a new business
Shifting house
Beginning a new intimate relationship
Taking up a course of study
Being involved in friends' problems
Managing a baby

Events affecting your household or family members
Facing a court case
Becoming handicapped or deformed
Becoming mentally disturbed
Undergoing a serious illness
Getting into trouble with the law
Starting a new job
Moving away from home
Having an accident
Losing a job
Starting school
Changing schools
Taking up a part-time course of study.

Are there any special events not mentioned here which you recognise as potentially increasing the tension in your life? Write them down.

What action will you take to care for your health this week?

EXERCISE
Sources of stress we take for granted
Apart from the major events outlined in the previous exercise other experiences may contribute to increasing our tension levels. Some of these situations may be occurring to us regularly without us being aware of the effects they are having on our bodies. Tick any of those which affect you at present.
- Do you work in a noisy environment, in inadequate lighting or in a room with poor ventilation?
- Do you work too close to other people?
- Do you stand or sit for hours at a time?
- Do you feel you have to do things most of the time rather than wanting to do them?
- Are you always being pushed to meet time deadlines?
- Are you expected to produce outstanding performances all the time?
- Is it a long time since you had a holiday or a break?
- Are you working longer hours and getting less time for leisure?
- Are your work companions always serious?
- Do you work with or often meet with people who have many personal problems?
- Does your work need fine physical co-ordination?
- Do your tasks require a lot of visual work?
- Do you live or work with people who are tense and always in a hurry?
- Are you getting too little sleep?
- Is your diet inadequate?
- Do you smoke?
- Do you drink too much alcohol?
- Are you not exercising enough to release tension?
- Is there conflict in your marriage or relationships?
- Do you have unresolved psychological conflicts with your family or people you live or work with?
- Is your current financial state perilous?
- Do you have on-going low self-esteem?

THE NEW YOU

> - Do you find it difficult to express your anger or other feelings?
> - Do you get little recognition for your efforts?
>
> Consider what you could do to change these conditions or how you could lessen the stress they cause you.

Aids to stress management

Recognising you may be under a lot of tension means you have come halfway to doing something about it. There is no single solution for everyone. Some choose yoga or meditation to relax, tapping their internal sources of energy. Others find it difficult to relax through meditating but enjoy sport as a means of unwinding. You may find that developing better breathing habits and a more balanced diet are the most useful ways for you to relieve tension.

Relaxation to reduce the effects of stress

Herbert Benson and Miriam Z Klipper have written an interesting book which explores the need for people, especially city dwellers, to find ways of avoiding some of the effects of daily stress.[4]

Looking at the increase in the United States of younger people suffering from high blood pressure and heart attacks, the authors found that meditation was one means of changing behaviour to overcome the symptoms of stress. They conclude that the 'Relaxation Response' is a natural gift which all of us have the possibility of developing. It is a universal human capacity developed through various religious, philosophical and tribal practices with which we have often lost touch in our modern lives.

Regardless of the cultural source of the experiences people have had in altering their consciousness, there are four elements of the 'Relaxation Response':
- Seeking a quiet environment where you can 'turn off' from outside distractions.

- Finding a comfortable position you can maintain for about 20 minutes. This is usually sitting rather than lying down as the aim of the exercise is to induce deep relaxation rather than sleep.
- Having a mental device to dwell on which helps to clear the mind by concentrating on, say, a word or sound repeated, gazing at an object, or focusing on a particular feeling. This can also help to eliminate distracting thoughts.
- Developing a passive attitude. This means being able to empty all thoughts and distractions from your mind. This seems to be the most important factor. It means that you are relaxed about what you are doing so that you can allow thoughts or images to drift through your consciousness. You do not concern yourself with how well you are doing in this process. Like all new skills keep at it and do not be upset if it takes some time to master. The results may reduce your blood pressure levels and increase your lifespan.

Guidelines for exercising

Consciously choosing to introduce more physical exercise into your life may assist you to unwind. Here are some general guidelines for selecting your kind of exercise:
- Check with your doctor before starting a fitness program.
- Choose something you enjoy.
- Choose a time of the day to suit your lifestyle.
- Allow time to warm up and cool down after exercise.
- Do too little rather than too much.
- Do not exercise when you are ill.
- Be guided by your heart rate or pulse. If you cannot comfortably talk or whistle while exercising you are pushing too hard.
- Do stretching exercises smoothly and slowly to avoid injury.
- Do not exercise straight after a meal or after drinking alcohol.
- Set yourself attainable short-term goals.

- Exercise with a friend and in pleasant surroundings.
- Record your progress and enjoy your achievements.
- Think pleasant thoughts.
- Sing to yourself or play music.

Rest before you reach burnout
Burnout happens when a person lets the desire to succeed at everything over-rule the need to enjoy life. It is something that can afflict women who are intensely involved in proving they are excellent in all their roles as career-woman, lover, housekeeper and mother.

The main message for those who could be susceptible to burnout seems to be that you learn to take note of what your natural rhythms are – and let them guide you to ease off and bring some balance back into your life.

My idea of success is to keep a balance so that we can enjoy what we do and be happy about ourselves and our activities. Feeling successful means being aware of burnout and realising it may lead to us not being able to feel anything at all unless we heed what our bodies tell us when we feel pushed and exhausted.

Are you beginning to feel compulsive about your job and your other roles in your crowded life without feeling any of the initial zest and *joie de vivre* you once prized? Now could be a good time to ease off and listen to what your body is telling you.

When you recognise that you are neglecting the mundane tasks of living such as paying bills, getting dry-cleaning done, remembering people's birthdays as well as depriving yourself of enjoying the time spent with your loved ones, you need to slow down and work on an action plan for you.

If you do not slow down you could become chronically exhausted, and lose contact with yourself, gradually depriving yourself of being able to feel anything at all emotionally.

Maybe it is time for you to stop denying yourself a restful holiday, particularly if you are the kind of person who never takes time off for a break. Once you are not exhausted you can begin to get some perspective back into your life.

Other basics like the power of breathing properly and a good diet are things which we can learn to be more careful about. Feeling alive with lots of energy is a very precious sensation. Striving to achieve that for ourselves is in itself worth feeling successful about.

Breathing and other basics
General health guidelines suggest taking five deep breaths outdoors each day, emptying your lungs in order to aid your concentration and mental effort through increasing the absorption of adequate oxygen in to your lungs.

Breathing is very important to us. We often make our state of anxiety worse by too much breathing or the wrong kind. Learning to control our breathing can be very helpful in enabling us to relax under tension.

As part of learning relaxation techniques we realise that distress, tension and panic often make us gulp, fight for air or catch our breath which results in too much oxygen being taken into the body.

This kind of panic breathing can then lead to physical symptoms associated with heart failure, headaches, dizziness, fainting, visual problems, and tingling and numbness of the feet and hands. Often this is due to breathing heavily with the top third of the lung and upper chest rather than breathing out using the lower part of the lungs and slowing down the rate. Learning to breath slowly using the bottom part of the lungs enables us to cope better with distress and tension. Some of us may already be familiar with these methods as they are similar to techniques used in natural childbirth.

On a more advanced level yoga can be very useful in teaching varied types of breathing to assist the body to achieve deep physical relaxation and heightened spiritual awareness. These techniques can be learnt from teachers, from books or from tapes.

Recognising when we are feeling under panic, or very stressed and then taking the time to control our breathing to calm ourselves is part of learning stress management.

One of the other very effective means of controlling our tension level is to talk positively to ourselves. Sometimes we need to be able to raise our self-image after a verbal side-swipe by someone we live with or work alongside.

Recognising our intrinsic worth as people who may not often get recognition or encouragement for our efforts can begin to assist our self-esteem. Self-talk can be very beneficial here to clear away some of the self-imposed tension.

EXERCISE
Coping with the rate of change
Tick any of those which you have experienced recently.
- feeling ambivalent about what is happening to you
- finding that your family is afraid of the 'new you'
- realising that the children do not see any benefits to them in what you are doing
- seeing that your husband or partner is putting up a lot of resistance to your plans even though they have not really started yet
- needing to make more space for yourself
- difficulty in coping with all you have to do in a day
- signs of feeling under stress
- signs of burnout
- other signs which you need to monitor
- experiencing several major stressful events over the past two years

Now write down what action you can take to live more comfortably with the 'new you'. Set out your own goals to improve your situation with action dates (see Chapter Five) and review how you are feeling in a month's time.

THE NEW YOU

Remember the words of Desiderata: 'Be gentle with yourself ... Many fears are born of fatigue and loneliness ... You have a right to be here ... In the noisy confusion of life keep peace with your soul ... Strive to be happy.'

PART II

MOVING FURTHER IN

9 HOW FAR DO YOU WANT TO GROW?

'No woman in my time will be Prime Minister or Chancellor or Foreign Secretary – not the top jobs. Anyway I wouldn't want to be Prime Minister. You have to give yourself 100 per cent.'

This was a statement made by Margaret Thatcher, in an interview in the *Sunday Telegraph* on 26 October 1969, on her appointment as Shadow Education Spokesman. Why did she change her mind?

I would suggest that Mrs Thatcher, like so many women, did not realise how far she could go until she started on her journey. We are, after all, entitled to change our minds and set ourselves extraordinarily ambitious goals as we get older.

How many of you have set yourself goals and then been surprised when you have reached them much earlier than you had expected? Then you find new goals, new targets to aim for, new challenges to meet. If you sometimes think you are limited in what you can do, read Margaret Thatcher's statement and start to think again.

Now is the time for you to dream and aspire further than you might have dared to in the past. If you are daunted by the amount of learning you might have to do to reach your goal remember to give yourself realistic dates to make it by – allow yourself five years to set up your own business or organisation, or become president of a council, or devote yourself mostly to painting, or finish that degree course you have hankered after, or tour around Australia, or retire gracefully to a flower farm, or become shire mayor, or conductor of the orchestra, or head of your own department. This five year plan then allows you to work backwards on an action plan.

> **EXERCISE**
> **Daring to Dream**
> Write down your dream goals – the ones you were too conservative or sensible or practical or unsure of yourself to indulge in earlier. Then read on to find out how much capacity you have to realise them.

A starting point

Research has shown that certain qualities are <u>indicators of a person's capacity to grow</u>. If we do not have these capacities to a marked degree at present we can develop them as part of our decision to grow. Some of them need practice in order to develop. Some of them may form the basis of skills we decide to work on for the rest of our lives.

> **EXERCISE**
> **Assessing your capacity to grow**
> Read through the following sections and think about them in terms of your recent life. Then note down in your private book those areas you might seek to develop or work on or change.
>   Set yourself some goals arising from your resolutions in particular areas and follow up with specific action plans. Work out how you will be able to measure even a small achievement in what you have set yourself.

How adaptable are you?

Are you receptive to gaining and assimilating a wider range of information about:
- yourself?
- other people?
- groups or work situations you belong to?

- your own society?
- other societies?
- your physical environment?

Are you willing to take on new roles?
How do you react to new freedoms, new obligations and new responsibilities?
How flexible are you?
Are you able to retain your intellectual and moral integrity and still modify your ideas and beliefs?
Are you able to change your personal norms and emotional attachments while still maintaining your moral and intellectual integrity?

A useful way of finding out about other people is to join a group, either for work, interest or relaxation and start to look at the world from the group's point of view.

I had the opportunity of doing this early in my life when I lived in another country. More recently I have had the opportunity of working with committees made up of varied people committed to the same goals. Doing this may be one of your first steps in learning about different views of the world and becoming more flexible in the process. It can be a stimulating way of beginning to grow.

Are you able to attain goals you set yourself?

Do you have the capacity to postpone getting some of the things you would like now in order to achieve longer term desires?
Are you able to conceive of a growing number of ways in which you could find satisfaction in your life?
Are you able to assess and evaluate which of those possible ways you might pursue?
Can you cut out your commitment to one goal and transfer that commitment to new, additional ones when necessary?
Can you learn how to attain those goals even if it takes you along new and different paths?

How integrated are you as a person?
How sure are you of your identity?
Are you able to perform a growing number of different roles without losing your identity?
Can you undertake an increasing variety of social relationships without suffering the diffusion of your identity?

How far can you go in your involvement with others?
Are you developing the capacity to get more deeply involved emotionally with others without surrendering your self?
Are you increasing your ability to convey your experience, learning and capabilities to others?

Know yourself
Finding out information and being ready to consider it is one of the easiest steps people can make when beginning to take action to achieve goals.

If you have read Part I of this book you have probably already found out quite a bit more about yourself than you knew in the beginning.

Being open to increasing knowledge about yourself is, I believe, very empowering for people. Once you recognise certain patterns of behaviour you have adopted in the past you can choose to change or accept them depending on what you want in the future.

Chart the world around you
Gathering information about other areas of our lives can also be a way of challenging our prejudices and opening the door to new possibilities. If you are trying to persuade others to take a new path or consider new ideas, you will find that well-prepared information is one of the most effective ways to bolster your argument.

The term 'mapping' describes how we organise our perceptions and understandings of the world with our individual beliefs and interests. Our 'maps' can be priceless guides for us but they can often become rigid and confining. This can limit our perceptions and thus limit our ability to grow and cope with change.

Perhaps you will find it useful to explore your own conceptual map and decide whether you need to gradually develop a different map or enlarge your present one.

How many roles do you play?
In the past it has been noted that women are often not able to see themselves in new roles in their paid work situations. This helps to explain the small number of women who volunteer to do training courses within organisations, or who join committees within professional organisations. It also explains why many very competent women do not apply for jobs they have the capacity and experience to do.

Deciding to grow may lead you to consider what different roles you could take on and then take the necessary steps to make that happen.

Take a positive attitude towards criticism
One of the hardest things for a lot of women to learn is to accept objectively assessment or criticism about their work. Sadly, many accept the criticism as a judgment of themselves as people rather than using the information to begin to change their behaviour and thus become more competent in their job.

Learning to be more objective about suggestions and criticism may help you to change your ideas without feeling you personally are in danger of disintegrating. In this way you can continue to grow.

Goals and integration
Earlier in this book we discussed setting and attaining goals. By now you are probably in touch with your ability to handle goals. Keep on working at it. The skills become easier as you keep trying and learning.

Establish your self-image

In order to increase your capacity for change you need to have a fairly clear picture of who you are and who you want to be. Gathering knowledge about yourself and accepting it can help you a lot. Other people can be very good in giving you valuable feedback about yourself. Sometimes you need to temper what they say with why they say it. But an objective discussion with a perceptive person familiar with how you operate in groups or at work can be very useful and revealing about you as a person.

Understanding that you have both strengths and weaknesses does not mean that you have to broadcast them to others either. We are talking about self-image here! Once you have a clearer image of the kind of person you are you can begin to develop the self-confidence to act on that self-image and open yourself up to change without threatening yourself.

With increased self-confidence you can step into new situations and test them against what you want to be able to do in your future life. You can always choose not to pursue particular paths if they are not suited to your self-image.

Or you may realise that you can perform in new roles if you develop new techniques for working with groups. For example, many women who are appointed to committees, councils or boards feel a conflict between how they would prefer to act and how the group is used to acting, particularly if the group plays politics and is used to a power model of decision making.

You can develop techniques to help you cope with these situations that do not undermine your self-image, if your stance is one you wish to keep. We discuss more about these differences in Chapter 13.

Self versus others

The idea of becoming emotionally involved with others without surrendering yourself is one that hits at the heart of self-development for most women. I believe many women want to be able to develop their self-image, and at the same time be intimate with a partner or husband and enjoy friendships on various levels. They wish to feel individual without feeling they have to give up their 'oneness' to love others.

In a reassessment of a relationship this issue is very important, especially if the partners are at different stages of growth and are used to a traditional husband–wife model where the wife accepts the husband's ideas, does little questioning of his decision-making role in the family and has been prepared in the past to be mainly a domestic support person backing up his career and his role as the sole bread-winner of the family.

Interpersonal competence

Alice Sargent has developed the idea of measuring interpersonal competency skills along a scale.[1] I have used her material as the basis of an exercise in which you begin to assess your own skills. There are no values attached to any of the points along the scales because the skills mentioned may be appropriate at different times and in different situations in our lives.

I believe that part of our ability is to recognise the skills we already possess and those we might want to develop. We all need interpersonal skills no matter what roles we play in life.

Sometimes the most painful part of learning is knowing which skill we should have used or might have used in a particular situation. This often becomes obvious only after the event. When this happens it is probably important to reflect on what action or stance might have been more appropriate and to resolve to try to do that next time we get into a similar position.

<u>A person's confidence and feelings of personal power increase as he or she is able to freely select from a number of different skills in any situation.</u>

> **EXERCISE**
> **Interpersonal competence**
> Have a look at the following eight areas and think about how you interact with people in various situations. Mark with a tick (✓) if you already have this skill. Mark with a cross (x) where you have no skills. Put a star (★) beside the areas where you would like to improve your skills.
>
> You may be lucky enough to already be able to tick most of the points along each scale. Ideally you will grow in competence so that you can eventually tick each point because you are able to select any behaviour appropriate to your situations.

Leadership

One of the most valuable skills a woman can learn is assertiveness expressing clearly what you would like to do or prefer to happen in a situation in which you are involved.

Assertiveness is essential if we are to learn to rebel against taking commands when we regard those commands as inappropriate, unjust, unbearable or frankly unworkable.

At the other end of the scale learning to be assertive can enable us to take command when the situation calls for it. This may follow on from deciding to reject someone else's commands. Or it may be a situation in which we should take command for our own good and that of our ideals. Or it may simply be essential to take command in order to prove we can do it as part of our career path.

Learning to follow command, compromise and help others to take command are more subtle skills. It can be very difficult for people who are strongly power-oriented to learn these three skills. For them it is often easier to reject someone else's authority and take control themselves than to learn to work under others.

HOW FAR DO YOU WANT TO GROW?

Leadership				
Take command	Help others take command	Compromise	Follow command	Rebel against taking commands
Visibility				
Centre stage	On stage	Backstage	Observe at a distance	Be absent
Group size and ease of participation				
Large groups	Small groups	Pairs and couples	Individuals	Alone
Conflict and confrontation				
Generate	React to	Mediate	Ignore	Avoid
Ability to link in with others				
Intimate	United	Teammate	Distant	Isolated
Helper/Helpee				
Express vulnerability	Take suggestions; get feedback	Share support	Give help	Rescue others
Self-disclosure (revealing your self and your experiences)				
Disclose self	Hint at openness	Present facade	Hide	Disappear
Limits and controls				
Set and keep strong limits	Suggest limits	Develop limits	Test limits	Break limits

Reprinted by permission of the publisher, from *The Androgynous Manager* by Alice G Sargent, page 68, © 1983 AMACOM, a division of American Management Associations, New York. All rights reserved.

In developing organisations with growth potential one of the most important skills is being able to compromise when necessary. This skill is also required in running a household.

Being able to help others to take command when appropriate, enables us to allow others to develop their ideas and take credit for them. This is a very valuable skill to have in situations requiring new ideas, new ways, new solutions to improve existing methods or to develop potential opportunities.

Visibility

The degree to which we choose to be visible or invisible is of course linked to leadership. If we choose to be on centre stage for most of our lives we will have trouble ever helping others to take command unless they are supporting our high visibility.

Similarly it is a very confident person who can develop something behind the lines and actually observe at a distance. Perhaps the most confident person of all is the one who can trust others sufficiently to do things in his or her absence.

Entrepreneur, Lore Harp, set up a business in her kitchen in 1976. She is now the managing director of 'Vector Graphic' a United States company worth $25 million. She says she likes to hold loose reins over people and give them the responsibility of letting them do their own jobs. The ultimate example she gives of this is that she seldom calls the office to see how things are going when she is out of town.

On the other hand, some of us may recognise that our standard visibility positions have always been backstage. We have taken the role of always being part of a team, backing up others, contributing to projects without having our efforts recognised or being seen as contributing to the show.

It may be that this area needs developing in order for you to be where you want to be in five years' time. Now

HOW FAR DO YOU WANT TO GROW?

may be the time to consider if this is one of the areas you could work on to enable you to grow into a more confident person when you have to stand in the limelight.

Another skill related to this might be learning to speak confidently in public. Doing a public speaking course is a wonderful way of gaining confidence in simply expressing what you want to say.

Group size and ease of participation

Considering our level of comfort with different groups is very interesting. On the one hand, I believe it is essential for us to feel comfortable when we are alone – feeling at home with yourself may be a skill you need to develop if you have always sought to be with other people and hated ever being by yourself. On the other hand, feeling confident with big groups of people can be very reassuring when we have to attend meetings or conferences.

Being able to relate to another person one-to-one is important in managing people and being able to communicate with them. It may take a bit of thought and practice if you are the kind of person who has always felt ill-at-ease with just one other person, but is well worth developing as part of being able to grow.

Women are often more competent in participating with individuals or pairs and couples than in larger groups. Their experience has prepared them more for getting on with people in familiar informal situations or as professionals in one-to-one situations than in larger groups.

Recognising that you are not able to participate easily in large groups is the first step towards developing your large group skills. A public speaking course may help you to feel more at ease with large numbers of people. Similarly you may want to develop your small group skills if you do not feel comfortable working with a team, committee, council or board.

Conflict and confrontation

This is one area where many of us have to face our past

attitudes and realise they may not be adequate to enable us to grow in the future.

How many of us say we hate conflict?

How many of us realise we may need to occasionally generate conflict in order to have our ideas listened to and heard? Will we learn to mediate and negotiate rather than avoid or ignore conflict at work or in our homes?

Can we learn to react to conflict, to fight back when we are confronted rather than wanting always to back down? Learning to recognise what we want to achieve in a particular situation, being very well prepared, asserting ourselves, and being brave will help us to move to a freer position in confronting and negotiating when we need to. Living with a family gives us a lot of scope for practice in this area.

Linking with others, being a helper/helpee and self-disclosure

Our ability to isolate ourselves or be distant when necessary, to be part of a team, intimate or united when appropriate, is closely linked to our helper/helpee roles and our ability to disclose ourselves to others if we choose.

If we are always getting involved in helping others through their personal crises but do not want to do this all our lives we may need to learn skills in becoming more isolated or distant from people we do not want to have leaning on us any more. This may mean not seeing ourselves as everyone's helper in life.

We may need to learn to present a facade of not caring as much about people as we have in the past in order to survive and grow in different directions. Or we may seek to share support rather than always feeling obliged to do a 'rescue job' ourselves when someone calls on us for help.

One way of being part of a more united group may be to learn to admit your vulnerability. You do not have to have all the answers all the time. Telling people you do not know how to do something, asking for suggestions and looking for support may be skills we need for our ongoing growth.

In the workplace many of us need to learn when it is appropriate to express our vulnerability and when it is not. Too many of us are used to confessing our weaknesses and inner struggles without giving the whole picture of our strengths and our convictions as well. Often we learn later that the person we confided in betrayed our confidence or was not able to recognise it for what it was.

Some of us need to be more distant, to present facades of competence and confidence even when we are feeling insecure and vulnerable. We should not feel obliged to disclose ourselves unless we are convinced that it will not be taken as a sign of weakness by those we are dealing with.

If we are moving into new areas of interest it is especially important to stand back for a while and learn who to trust and how far to go before we are our trusting, open selves.

Being able to choose which level of self-disclosure is suitable and appropriate, where to be intimate and where to be distant, when to give help and when to accept it makes a person rich in interpersonal skills. Only after much experience and with great self-confidence are we able to <u>know</u> exactly which level is appropriate for a particular situation.

Training and helping others

Once we feel secure within ourselves and have developed our self-confidence we are prepared to share our knowledge and experience with others.

Although many women are initially attracted or directed to teaching as a career, this is not the same as sharing our learning with others. Rather, this notion applies to a willingness to assist other adults or children when they ask for assistance or when they need your experience if you are responsible for them.

There are a myriad of ways we can share knowledge and learn other than in the traditional classroom or lecture. Just being prepared to talk to someone on an individual basis about how you dealt with an issue similar to hers or his is the kind of sharing of knowledge that a mature person may choose as part of growth.

Testing your learning style

You may find it useful at some stage to test your dominant learning style so that you can increase your capacity to learn and to convey your knowledge to those around you.

One of the interesting ways of doing this is to buy a copy of the *Learning Style Inventory*, available from local suppliers of training equipment.[2]

The *Learning Style Inventory* is based on experiential learning theories and shows us whether we favour a particular style of learning that may not be sufficient for us to broaden our knowledge in the future.

The idea of learning is not restricted to the limited educational sense of learning. It extends to the broader adaptation-to-life aspects, including decision-making, problem-solving and lifestyles in general.

For example, I found that learning from watching and observing others has been useful to me in my business. This method is seldom discussed as a practical method of 'on the job' training. But it is the cheapest and simplest way to pick up a lot of practical ideas and business background.

Another underrated method is learning by doing. Again this is the 'on the job' training every person in any kind of supervisory or managerial role has experienced. We learn to be mothers more through experience than training. Similarly, we can go on to develop new skills in other jobs by 'having a go'. Once we increase our awareness of needing to learn by experience we can look openly for ways of doing this more often.

The *Learning Style Inventory* itself assumes that any of the four basic styles it describes are valid ways of learning. However it is based on the concept that the most effective learning will include some of the four areas of skills and that learning styles are not fixed forever. They can change as people choose to learn differently.

If you find that you are very low in one or two styles of learning, you might decide to develop other ways of learning in the future.

It can also be a useful way of exploring how best to teach people in a course or people who work with you, especially if you are finding that you are not communicating well with them at present. Perhaps you are relying on a particular learning style which a number of your group do not favour. Recognising this could enable you to consider other methods of communication or training.

Further study

While we are talking about learning styles let us look at the place of further study in your plans to grow.

Maxine decided she wanted to learn about computers and find a job in that field. She discovered that she could do a post-graduate diploma which gave her an excellent introduction to how computers work, an overview of several different computer languages, and dealt with some of the issues of using computers in organisations. This diploma was open to people who already had a degree but was not restricted to people having only a science or mathematics background.

After Maxine had finished her diploma she got a job which led to her setting up an Information Centre for assisting employees to effectively use micro-computers in their work. Maxine was particularly suited to running this centre as she could combine her knowledge with her ability to understand what people needed to learn about micro-computers in particular.

On the other hand, Trudie was very disillusioned after working in a highly technical position for a number of years. Although she was the first woman to attain some of her specialist qualifications and she worked well in the position, she found that the job was not satisfying her needs.

Trudie decided to do a course which would lead her into business. She chose a Secretarial Diploma.

Because she was used to a high degree of autonomy in her earlier jobs Trudie found it very difficult to settle down to being a personal assistant. Her typing and shorthand were excellent but she resented having to do that kind of work all day. She also found it very demeaning to have to serve cups of tea and coffee to her boss and his associates.

Finally Trudie went into her own business as manager. This suited her much better. With hindsight and given her obvious ability she probably should have chosen a Master of Business Administration or a Diploma of Marketing or a similar course. As a result she would have looked for quite different jobs and have found them more rewarding. Also those courses would have given her an excellent background later in her own business.

Choose a worthwhile course for job prospects

If you have as a goal the need to get a rewarding job or the need to be able to earn money to keep a family, then one of your action points will probably be to do extra study. I certainly encourage you to take this on. But do not spend all that effort and hardship on a degree or diploma which will not help you to achieve your goals.

Think carefully before you commit yourself to studying for a course such as a diploma or degree which involves an incredible amount of commitment, effort and organisation over a number of years.

As an employer I have had several applications from women who have worked as secretaries in their early years, given up work to have children, studied for university degrees as mature-age students, and then gone back seeking jobs. These women were looking for the kind of job we were offering because they wanted more than just secretarial work but the subjects they had studied appeared to be of no use to our job requirements. In fact they suggested to us that the women were probably not interested in our kind of work at all.

Let me explain this in a bit more detail from the point of view of an employer. The particular job we were looking to fill required some secretarial skills, but it also needed someone able to take initiative, research various business subjects and prepare reports when necessary. It had the potential to be an interesting job and could have given the right woman the chance to eventually move into other areas of business.

From our point of view we wanted someone who showed evidence of being interested in business, who perhaps read some of the business papers and who was competent. We were disappointed when we looked at the applications from the women who had had excellent experience in their previous jobs as secretaries but had then studied for their Bachelor of Arts with no business subjects at all and no sign of an interest in business in their reading or hobbies.

What point is there in interviewing a woman who says she wants to work in business but has not chosen to study any subjects such as economics, marketing, accountancy, business studies, or computing? If you want to put so much energy into learning about art, history, psychology, social or political sciences, fine arts or learning another language please make sure of your reasons for your choice of subjects.

While many of these subjects may be appropriate for certain jobs or for acquiring general knowledge for its own sake, do be sure that is why you are doing it. If you want to study in order to get back into the workplace or to further your chances of success in your career it is worthwhile checking to be sure you will spend your precious energy acquiring knowledge relevant and useful in the area you may have to work in eventually. Otherwise I believe you are sabotaging your chances of success in your future paid working life.

Too often women graduates who are looking at broadening their career paths choose a post-graduate diploma or degree in secretarial studies rather than a more ambitious course in marketing, computers or management. Did you know that one of the main qualifications to be considered for a Master of Business Administration is having an excellent first degree in virtually any discipline?

If you want to change your career directions, look to more than a secretarial role. If you have had experience doing anything in a professional capacity you will not want to be ground down in a support role for many years hoping for an opening to arrive. You will have much more chance of finding openings in organisations with a broader course of study to support typing skills, if necessary.

I believe that if you choose to do a secretarial course for your second degree or diploma you are telling employers that this is what you want to do with your life. If you choose instead to do a course in management or business studies you are giving a very different message to employers about where you want to go in your career. I stress this merely as a means of encouraging you to spend your precious energy on useful ends. Fit your actions to attaining your goals.

EXERCISE
A goal review
In the light of this chapter get out your goals and action lists and review them.

Have you let your dreams go far enough? Will your current action plans enable you to grow? If you need to set new goals or to work out new action plans to position yourself to attain new skills do it now. Be realistic about allowing yourself time to increase your skills and potential.

Review your progress in six months' time. You may be surprised how far you have come in being able to grow both as a person and in your chosen career.

10 STRATEGIES AND SKILLS FOR YOU AND YOUR HOUSEHOLD

In this chapter I want to explore some of the issues that arise as a result of your decision to take on outside interests if you share a household with children, a husband or partner and possibly other family. Many of the issues are the same no matter what you decide to involve yourself in, ie creative activities, starting a business, taking up study, joining a group or committee or commencing paid work.

Any of these kinds of changes will affect you and your household in some way or another. Being aware of this can help you to discuss and plan so that the new era is ushered in with the minimum of problems.

What are the main issues?

Elsewhere in this book I have mentioned the difficulties many people have in adjusting to new situations and ideas. 'People' include our children, our partners, our parents and other family and friends. Other 'people' may even include our pets.

EXERCISE
How crowded is your life at present?
In this simple exercise you can begin to work out what time and emotional pressures people and things put on your life at present. The aim of the exercise is to enable you to realise what your current situation is. You can then consider whether you want to

change that situation and then <u>how</u> you can change it in order to have more space to grow.

You may need a big piece of paper or you may be able to write in small letters on a page or a double page of your own private book.

Try to look at yourself in the centre of, say, a small frame which is surrounded by two larger frames. This represents three levels of involvement of things, activities and people in your life.

You can now start thinking about how various things impinge on your life and where you place them in relation to yourself. The closer these are to you in the diagram the more pressure they put on you emotionally, or the more time they take up in your life.

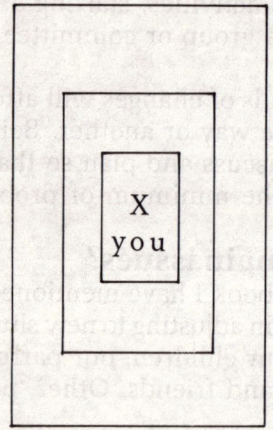

In general terms the central frame around you will contain the people, activities and things which take up a lot of your physical and emotional effort and time.

The middle frame will contain the ones which take up some of your efforts but are not as pressing or demanding. These are ones you can more easily postpone, change or fit in to meet your own requirements.

STRATEGIES AND SKILLS

The outside frame may include once a year events or activities, people who are of some influence on you or whose interest you have to consider to a lesser degree in the decisions you make.

Some of the most obvious ones to put in the central frame are your children, if you have any. How close you put them to you on the diagram at present will vary according to their ages, their dependence on you in various ways and perhaps your dependence on them for interests and companionship. If they have left home, they may fit in the middle or outer frame.

Other things associated with your children which you might include are their activities, meetings, sports, courses or training which require your time in providing transport or supervision and your encouragement.

Similarly your involvement with your partner or husband will determine how close that position is to yourself in the frame. If you have a very demanding job or boss or both, those things may go in the middle frame too. If you are already studying then that will go into one of the frames depending on your time and commitment to it. Maybe you look after elderly or sick relatives. In that case they may be close to you in the inner frame. If you have pets the position you put them in will depend on who looks after them and how much attention they require. And other people may impinge on your life if you have a lot of friends or employees who require various amounts of attention.

Activities must also be included. If you are heavily involved in an organisation you might place it in the central frame. If you do a fair bit of work for it you might place it in the middle frame. If it is not very demanding then it will go in the outside frame. If you spend a lot of time fighting for a cause or supporting a church group or a community project this will go in your central frame.

> If you are very happy with what you have found in your frames then you don't need to consider changing any positions. But if you have found that everything ended up in the inner frame, you might like to consider how to move some of them out a bit in order to allow yourself more time or space to grow. How you do this will depend on a lot of factors. You may simply need to be more ruthless with people who are imposing on you. Maybe you need to set yourself some times when no-one can disturb you. Or maybe you need to have a talk to the members of the household, especially if you are about to embark on new endeavours.
>
> You might regard this exercise as an initial audit of where your present efforts are spread in your life. It could be a good diagram to come back to in a year's time if you decide to branch out and grow on your own terms.

The issues involved in starting to study

Further study is an excellent way of preparing ourselves for a new direction in our careers. It may help us to update our knowledge or qualifications or it may simply give us a new interest in life. It also acts as a halfway step to paid jobs.

Many of the issues arising from a household adjusting to your being tied up with lectures, assignments and interests outside the house are the same as when you work part-time or full-time outside the house. The solutions members of the household find to problems in their new situations will help them to cope with more permanent situations later when work may well replace study as an ongoing part of your life.

We may commence study when our families are still young or we may wait till they are older and away at school during the day. And of course we can still choose to study when the children have produced grandchildren if we want to.

Studying with babies and young children

At a very successful conference run by Women in Management on 'Enterprising Women' some years ago it was suggested that women might consider studying to increase their qualifications while they look after young children at home. While this may not suit all women who are coping with demanding young families, it is a possibility you could consider particularly if some of them go to kindergarten or school.

I followed this path when I decided to do my postgraduate Diploma in Marketing. I began the course the year my son started kindergarten and had just enough time to prove to myself I could do it before our daughter arrived.

My son had four kindergarten sessions weekly of about three hours each. These periods of time were my main chance to read, study and do my assignments. I learnt to study intensively in short bursts and not to procrastinate about doing an assignment. My first assignment was the hardest. Studying early in the morning was also necessary as I often found I was too tired at night to settle down to the kind of reading I had to do.

Halfway through the second semester we adopted our daughter. Fitting a five-week-old baby into the system took a bit of doing at first. However, apart from handing in the only late assignment ever, things went fairly smoothly.

I confess my work never reached the zeniths of my first semester efforts. I became more ruthless through necessity about the time I could spend on assignments. And I learnt to work out ideas in my head while driving or doing the washing, which has been invaluable as a planning skill ever since.

Here are some helpful hints:
- Always plan to get your assignments finished well ahead of the due date.

- Consider getting someone else to type up your assignments if you can afford it.
- See if you can stretch the budget to get a person or cleaning service to do some of the heavy house cleaning for you a couple of hours a week.
- Try to have a few back-up friends or relatives to look after the children when they are sick or your partner is unavailable and you have to spend a few extra hours catching up on things.
- Look for council-provided services or a good crèche where you could leave a baby or child for a few hours or for a regular day a week to give you more time for uninterrupted study.
- Consider using a microwave oven, a bain-marie or some organised system of managing meals to cut out having to cook several times a night for young children and older people.

Probably the most important thing was organising to do my assignments well ahead of time. In a diary I marked down a date at least a week ahead for each assignment due and was careful to arrange for a typist in good time to type them once the material was ready.

Some of the least predictable events with young children are their various illnesses. I found that one way of coping with such unexpected problems was doing assignments ahead of time. This proved invaluable when, for example, the children got chicken pox and were quarantined for several weeks, tying me to the house.

Here are several other examples of women who decided to study while looking after babies.

Gita decided to up-grade her professional qualifications by studying for a diploma part-time while she was pregnant with her first child. Although she had a difficult pregnancy and was in hospital for several weeks before the baby was born she was able to apply for, and get, special consideration for a late assignment.

She continued with the course after she came home from hospital and took the baby along to lectures until it was old enough to be left with her husband or with friends.

Finally she earned her diploma and followed this with some part-time work under supervision to achieve full qualifications for her next professional stage. She was now ready to look at new avenues for work and interest once her child started school.

Lea, on the other hand, chose to study full-time for a new degree when her children were young. She was very aware that she had made the choice to leave some of the caring of her children to others including her mother, friends and a crèche. In her case she managed to complete her degree ready to begin an entirely new career when the children started school.

Choosing a course and subjects

Some courses are more demanding than others. Many academic and business courses require intensive assignments involving practical work. Often these assignments form part of the final assessment in the subject. High standards are also expected in order to obtain a pass.

This kind of information is worth finding out from both the staff running the courses and people (preferably women like yourself) who have taken the courses and have hands-on experience of how much time and effort was involved.

However, if a particular course will be invaluable to you later on, why not go ahead and do it anyway even if it takes twice as much effort as another less satisfactory one? If necessary you may need to ask for an extension to finish some subjects or convert from full-time to part-time study.

Do not ignore the opportunity which older children present when you need to learn skills in mathematics or other specialised subjects. Judith Ward found that her son was a patient and helpful teacher when she faced the task of learning mathematics after 25 years away from study.[1] *This encouraged her to begin with renewed enthusiasm her business studies by correspondence.*

There is no shame or problem about admitting that you took on too much too soon. It is still better to take five years to finish a useful course that others may do in three years, than to have not attempted it at all. The main thing is to safeguard yourself by making sure you are familiar with all the necessary junctures within which you have to apply for changes in your course, or whatever. These may be in your handbook or you can confirm these dates with a course co-ordinator.

Another point to consider when choosing subjects is what you would most like to do or what would be most useful to you. This is preferable to always letting the times of lectures determine whether you can fit in, say, collecting a child from school, with attending those lectures.

Part of taking control of your life is ensuring that you get the most out of the effort you are making to study. It is surprising how you can reach solutions to problems like subject times clashing with family duties once you start thinking more creatively or laterally.

The effect of studying on your marriage

Susan Kelly is a psychology lecturer who has completed a study on the impact of taking up studying on the marriages of a group of Australian women in their thirties.[2] The 40 women whom Kelly studied over a three-year period were aged between 30 and 40 and were enrolled at two large colleges of advanced education. They were mainly in full-time courses with no previous experience of higher education.

Both husbands and wives were interviewed separately in Kelly's research. Her findings showed that every marriage changed to some degree over the three-year period.

Kelly stressed that one of the positive results of the survey was the way in which all the women soared in confidence after returning to study. This improvement in self-confidence and happiness rubbed off on other family mem-

STRATEGIES AND SKILLS

bers, leading to an improved atmosphere in the home.

As far as the marriage relationships had suffered, 12 of the 40 had separated or divorced. However, on both marriage partners' assessments, 10 of the 40 reported considerable improvement and another two noted some improvement over the period of the study. Twelve of the marriages, originally ranging from satisfactory to good, reported little or no change in direction. Two marriages assessed from the start as 'devitalised' changed very little and two deteriorated somewhat but had not actually resulted in separation.

On the negative aspects of the wives' studying she found, not surprisingly, that couples had less time together at nights and weekends. Also the wives' increased knowledge and assertiveness sometimes led to more conflict, while their general fatigue and specific anxiety about tests and assignments added to general family stress levels.

Helping the family cope with mum's study

After summarising her findings Kelly had some useful suggestions about how to minimise the effects on the household of a wife and/or mother going back to study while still maximising her achievement and satisfaction.

One included the need for the household to view the woman's course of study as a joint project. This would apply equally to a wife and mother taking up paid work outside the house or starting a business or becoming involved in a community project.

Here are some suggestions for you to consider:
- Give people in the household a chance to know about what you are studying – be open with information and be prepared and ready to answer questions about what you actually do in the course of your day.
- Take the children along to the college or university for a meal or a visit or simply to the library when you are collecting a book. Take away some of the mystery of it all.
- Invite your husband to have lunch in the campus cafeteria with you and then let him sit in on a lecture with

you. Even if he does not take up the offer this may help to take away the fear of the unknown for him and allay his suspicions. If he does, he may be surprised at your courage in confronting the groups of younger students and have increased respect for your ability.
- Let your family meet some of the other people with whom you study. Maybe you could organise a barbecue or a social occasion for other families or couples to meet each other and share the experiences the men and women are facing in their changed lifestyles.
- Encourage the men to get used to spending more time with their children to avoid conflicts at crucial periods when essays or assignments are due in or when you have to study for exams. Renegotiate this whole area if necessary.
- Ignore early protests – fathers usually welcome the increased contact with the family and the chance to get closer to them. They also find that doing things with the children by themselves can lead to the development of special relationships and new shared interests. They can take the children to a movie mum is not interested in seeing, or to a sporting match or away camping. These become special experiences, different from the general family outings. Even preparing meals together can become a fun experience.
- Mothers might like to consider doing the same thing occasionally, if they have tended to do everything previously as a family. I have very warm memories of taking the children on bush walks, barbecues and to the snow by myself. I was also able to share with them what was going on, undistracted by another adult.
- All the evidence suggests that working women still do most of the housework. In the USA a working wife still does 26 hours compared to her husband's 36 minutes.[3] It will almost certainly be necessary to renegotiate who does what housework once you take up study or paid work. The whole family will have to take greater responsibility for various tasks or you will break under the

strain. We will talk about that in greater detail later.
- Work out ways in which your family life might be richer – even if it is not as often as you would like. Remember activities that the whole family enjoys – like playing games, going for picnics, going for bush walks or to the beach. Try to arrange that kind of special occasion for everyone at regular intervals and especially after you have finished an intensive assignment or exam. You can then give them all your undivided attention. It can help a family to cope with a great deal of stress and strain when they know the situation does not have to last forever and they have something to look forward to.

Useful skills for busy couples

When you develop other commitments outside the house whether they be study, community, self-development or paid work, you will find that you have new situations to deal with in your household.

These situations will revolve around more sharing of responsibilities for housework, looking after children, getting space to do things by yourself, being able to go out to meetings or lectures other than during school hours, coping with appointments and family crises, having more tense moments and so on.

These are the kinds of skills you will find very useful to brush up on or perhaps develop further through practice:
- regular communication with your partner
- regular communication with your children
- assertiveness
- problem-solving
- lateral thinking
- personal flexibility.

Communication covers a multitude of needs

Communication is a very complex process. Communicating with others includes talking, writing messages, deliberate actions and often unconscious gestures, 'body language' as it is popularly called.

Most of us have heard of the romantic notion of 'communication without words' – the idea of soul mates not needing to speak to each other, of each being so in tune with the other that needs are perceived and fulfilled without a word being spoken. I would suggest that if you did have this kind of silent communication with your husband or partner in the past, it is no longer enough in today's world once you start to take control of your life. Furthermore, this is precisely what many men think they lose when their wives move outside the house and are not around to wait on them after years of having anticipated their needs and fulfilled their expectations.

'Communication without words' also breaks down very fast when the man of your dreams indicates very clearly in words and deeds that you were not communicating to him at all because he was not able to perceive your need for fulfilment, creativity and self-esteem in all those years of your caring for him.

Ideally we can all learn to communicate much better with our families, and those with whom we associate. One of the skills required is simply being able to sit down or stand up or walk with others and talk with them about all kinds of things.

While we are still able to talk about things, we can develop methods of communicating better. Once we can no longer find the time or the emotional energy to talk to those we live with we will find it very difficult to work out some of the problems that arise from day to day and year to year.

Talking about sharing experiences and feelings

Women, overall, need to talk about how they feel and what they are doing in their lives more than men. The interesting issue that is now evident in modern marriages is the growing demand from women that partners be able to supply emotional support to each other rather than the more common situation of past decades when the husband expected and usually received emotional support from his wife but did not give much in return.

This came as something of a shock to men brought up in emotional straight-jackets. Admitting to themselves that they can feel emotions and are entitled to feel emotions without being unmanly is a big step for many men. Expressing these feelings to others, and being receptive to their feelings as well, is much further along the path to being vulnerable and taking emotional risks than many males are prepared to travel.

If intimacy is something you would like to develop in your relationship, its success will depend to a large extent on the ability of your husband or partner to adapt to that kind of change. Certainly it helps if you are able to share your experiences, both happy and unhappy, with your husband or partner.

This is particularly important in a family as it can give you a chance to sort out how you feel and get it out of your system. You can often start a 'new day' more easily with your children after you have reviewed their conflicts, problems or catastrophes with your husband at night.

Similarly there are times when everyone needs to discuss their own experiences outside the home with someone who cares about them. Feelings may mean joy or sorrow, hope or despair. Finding partners who will try to understand how we feel as well as expecting us to support them emotionally in return may not be easy.

If your husband or partner is not able to listen and understand your feelings, you may have to settle for finding or relying on good friends for support in that side of your life. However, communication covers much more than conveying feelings. Whatever you decide to do about your emotional needs you will still need to find effective ways of communicating about household arrangements once you become involved in study, work or other developments beyond the house.

STRATEGIES AND SKILLS

Talking about family manoeuvres
One of the main communication needs is to convey necessary information about what is happening to people when, how, and where. The most effective way is both to write down the information and speak about it directly to the person concerned. Of course the fewer links in the communication chain, the less distorted the message will be, so try to pass on the message yourself.

This particularly applies to messages about changes in routine and arrangements related to the basics of living such as eating, sleeping and travel (including picking up children from wherever they have been or conveying them to wherever they are supposed to be).

Lists, diaries, boards and the like
Many people use lists to keep communication lines flowing and to organise their lives. Having a board or a fixed place where everyone can write down what house and personal supplies are needed gives an immediate shopping list. It also enables people to say what they would like to have renewed without having to scream about it. The onus is on all household members to write up their requirements. Then whoever does the shopping has a ready-made shopping list.

Using message books and message boards can also be very useful in enabling the family to keep track of what the individuals are doing and to receive messages of various kinds. We use a special white board on the kitchen refrigerator to leave messages about where we have gone, what there is to eat, what needs to be done and reminders about where the children are located as well as for our shopping list.

We also have a diary reserved solely for phone messages about business or about personal matters. The most critical things about any diary or message book are:
- being able to find it
- remembering to write in the messages
- remembering to read it regularly.

While these may seem obvious they come back to the point I made that communication is most effective when it combines the written and the spoken word. Often a verbal reminder from the person who took the message reminds us to look at the message book.

Write it all down before you leave
I have learnt from experience that it is really worthwhile writing down as much as you can about things or changes in routine which may affect any member of the family. Then they can always refer to those written words of wisdom later when they have forgotten what you said to them.

If you are going away for a long period you would be wise to write down any information which may be needed from week to week. The degree of information needing to be documented at this stage depends on how much your household has learnt to fend for itself and how much they rely on you.

Some points may include:
- where you can be contacted
- children's school hours and how the children get there and back
- children's times for extra-curricular activities and transport arrangements
- feeding family and pets
- arrangements made for children's friends to play or stay
- phone numbers of friends
- phone numbers for emergencies.

There are other factors to be considered as well. If you have young children, you may need to write down considerable details about food routines, sleep routines, favourite toys and suggestions for play activities. Certainly these kinds of things help babysitters or temporary housekeepers or dads fit in better with the normal routine. Home minders also need to be told of any children's peculiarities such as bed-wetting, head-banging, food allergies and regular medication.

I have found that putting labels on children's drawers for their clothes has helped everyone – the housekeeper, the children and dad – to both put things away and find where they are when they are needed.

Older children can prove towers of strength by informing people of usual practices, habits and key locations for household items. They often have highly developed cooking skills and can be relied on to assist with chores beyond their normal responsibility. In fact your temporary absence may be a welcome developmental opportunity for your older children to show their capabilities.

Talking with your partner

When both you and your partner are busy, finding time to talk becomes much more difficult. But I believe it is essential to make time. There are many ways to do this. Some parents insist on time to themselves after a certain hour each night. Others book into their diaries lunches or dinners or days off or weekends away together so that they can catch up with each other. I particularly like the idea one woman executive has of meeting her husband regularly for a restaurant breakfast each week. Sometimes you can sneak in a pre-dinner drink by yourselves to catch up with the day if the children are watching television or playing in another room.

Another opportunity to talk together is when you are travelling together. Sometimes it is worthwhile driving each other to or from an appointment, or to an airport or a train station in order to have an uninterrupted talk.

Talking with the children

This raises several needs – those of the family sharing experiences together and those of the individual children getting a chance to talk to mum.

One of the main places for family members to get together is around the meal table. Although breakfasts are not very suitable occasions in our household, dinners at night are usually reserved for sharing with the children what they have done during the day and some of the things we have done as well. Sitting together and opening the way for conversation often allows the children to ask questions and explore issues together. This also gives us the opportunity to discuss what will happen in the coming week or in the holidays.

Going shopping, travelling in the car or playing with a child alone often presents the best opportunity to talk to the child by yourself. Even taking time in the evening to read a story, supervise homework, play a game or simply chat together with one child at a time can be very rewarding in keeping lines of communication open. You might not manage it every night but certainly trying to allow for the space a couple of nights a week is very worthwhile.

The other thing to consider in communication is how good you are as a listener when people talk to you. Do you hear what they are trying to tell you or are you busy trying to get only your message across?

This is especially important when your children talk to you. If you have less time with them than you used to, then you may need to work harder on picking up their real messages and the nuances of what they are saying and doing.

The other times to catch up with everyone are holidays. These can be very valuable as times for getting closer as a family and for sharing experiences and attention with individuals of the family. Again you may need to assert yourself and carve out space for this to happen, but holidays can be very useful in building up shared fun and experiences which the family members look back on with joy and happiness.

Assertiveness

There is no doubt that if you wish to survive in combining the roles of a wife and mother with those of a student and/or paid worker you will need excellent skills in asserting yourself. Put in its simplest form, 'assertiveness' is expressing your needs and wants without being destructive to other people.

Women often need to develop their ability to be assertive because they frequently know what they hope will happen but are constantly disappointed that other people do not perceive those hopes and make them happen. The commonest examples are about deciding where to go for an evening out. If you know what you want to do an assertive statement might be: 'I'd like to go to see the movie, *Stardust* on Saturday night. Would you like to come too?' In contrast an aggressive statement might be: 'You never take me out anywhere. I'm going to see *Stardust* on Saturday night whether you come or not.' A passive statement might be: 'Let's go out on Saturday night. What do you suggest we do?' Here of course the other person does not know that you want to see a movie, *Stardust*, because you have not given him or her that piece of information.

Of course being assertive does not mean you always have the solution to a problem. But it can open up the way for others to find solutions when you state what you want or what you need to do. Or it can lead to a satisfactory agreement or compromise between people once they are clear on what you want.

For example, if you realise you have an important assignment to finish over a weekend you might simply assert yourself at a family get-together by saying: 'I need to have the whole weekend free to finish my assignment. What can we do to make sure I get that time free?'

The way is then open for the family to make suggestions or to ask you for some suggestions: 'I don't want to cook any meals or do the washing. I would like you to get your own sandwiches for lunch and we'll get a takeaway meal for dinner. John and Sue can do the washing between them this weekend.'

STRATEGIES AND SKILLS

Solving problems, thinking laterally and being flexible

Solving problems often becomes possible when you think laterally and become more flexible. Of course it also helps if you are a trifle eccentric, were brought up in an untidy home, do not expect the world to be perfect and are very tolerant of grubby, fun-loving children and creative, absent-minded adults.

Since few of us share all of these attributes we quite often put up our own barriers to possible solutions to our problems, based partly on what we have been brought up to believe is the right and proper thing to do and partly on what we believe others will think of us if we do not do the right and proper thing.

Depending on the problem there are various ways of trying to solve it. One common phrase to use might be 'Who do we know who could help', if there are clashes in appointments, late night meetings or problems with sick children or holidays. In my case, this has led to developing close links with a reliable babysitting agency, various independent babysitters, friends, neighbours and relatives over the years.

I have also found council-run holiday programs excellent when I needed to spend some time in another area of the city on business.

I have found that it is often possible to combine business and family when necessary. We all spent an enjoyable weekend once at a seaside motel where I was a group leader for a live-in seminar. The seminar organisers arranged for a babysitter to entertain my children and several other children of participants. The whole occasion worked out very well for all of us.

On other occasions I have taken a single child to an official opening of a factory, to an official lunch or to a meeting when the child has not been very well. The children take a game to play or something to entertain themselves with and actually enjoy the outings as special occasions.

You may be lucky to have the kind of job where children who are sick or on holidays can be taken along without interrupting things too much. Increasingly I believe we should try to integrate children into our workplaces. This is partly so that we can break down some of the barriers between work and home, adults and children, and partly so that children themselves learn more about what work means for their parents – and later for themselves. I have found that both our children enjoy seeing where we work and associate buildings they have visited with their parents' places of work. The children are also interested in what we do and like to have discussions about current events that are taking place at work. It has been extremely rewarding taking the time to explain to them what we do and thus gain their interest and understanding.

Other problems call for different approaches. When things appear difficult a very useful question is: 'What is the worst that can happen to us?'. Once you work this out you can then look for a solution to that worst outcome and work backwards for less critical outcomes. This also has the benefit of putting things in perspective. If you are under stress in a crisis, facing the worst often calms you down because you realise you can cope with it. And it is very likely that you will not have to cope with the very worst.

Finally, one solution to a problem might be to do nothing. Some problems have a habit of not being the nuisance they promised to be, or of curing themselves with time. Making a decision to do nothing, at least for a time, can often be the best solution to problems in a family.

Making a household work
No chapter of this kind would be complete without a

STRATEGIES AND SKILLS

specific mention of how to share a household. As your career path opens up you may find the issue of housework becomes more urgent or more of a thorn in your side.

In order to achieve more harmony in a household, couples need to change their expectations about what will get done and about who will do it. Couples also need to accept that there are permanent changes in living and spending patterns once both partners work outside the home.

Most people agree that any change in the division of household tasks causes serious strain in the household in the beginning. The men may feel threatened and may resent having to do mundane, boring tasks. On the other hand, women have to adjust to giving up their territory. Some women enjoy having the role of housekeeper to themselves and once they share it they feel guilty or resentful that some of their role has been taken over by another person. They may feel jealous if the husband proves to be an excellent cook or can do the cleaning or washing better than they can or manage the children well.

Although dividing up the housework can be threatening to a woman, the alternative of trying to be the superwoman may result in a breakdown of the marriage or the woman's health. Role-sharing does eventually bring about increased empathy for one's partner. By actually taking over a job a person begins to understand and appreciate how much effort goes into doing it. This can bring couples closer together once the husband realises what his wife has done over the years and the wife can appreciate that he does understand.

Most two-career couples agree that lowering their standards of home care is essential. But men often only come to this conclusion once they have realised it is not worth the effort it takes to keep a house spotless. In the end the house may have to be a bit more untidy and a bit dirtier if the couple are to relax and spend an evening together.

STRATEGIES AND SKILLS

EXERCISE
Household tasks
Ideally you should do this as a whole family. Write down all the tasks that have to be done as part of managing your household. Here are some suggestions. You can add your own and cut out ones that do not apply to you.

Meals
- Cooking meals
- Preparing foods, salads, cutting vegetables
- Setting the table
- Clearing away the dishes
- Making lunches

Shopping
- Preparing lists
- Doing the supermarket shopping
- Doing other shopping, eg drycleaning, buying shoes, clothes for children, household maintenance

Garbage
- Taking bins out and in

Laundry
- Washing clothes, sheets, towels
- Drying/hanging out washing
- Bringing in washing
- Folding and sorting laundry
- Putting away clothes and linen
- Ironing
- Mending
- Arranging drycleaning

Garden
- Mowing lawns
- Weeding
- Keeping yard tidy
- Pruning trees

Cars
- Maintenance
- Getting petrol

Pets
- Feeding pets
- Taking pets to the vet

Cleaning
- Vacuuming
- Washing floors
- Cleaning bathrooms and toilets
- Washing windows

Repairs and maintenance
- Arranging for maintenance
- Buying tools, supplies, etc

Money
- Budget planning
- Bill paying
- Bank accounts
- Arranging mortgage payments, etc

Children
- Meetings at school
- Arranging transport
- Extra curricular activities
- Help with homework
- Organising babysitters
- Arranging visits to and from friends

Social obligations
- Family functions and obligations
- Gift buying
- Entertaining

Leisure
- Planning social activities
- Arranging holidays
- Weekend activities

1   Now have a good look at the list and cross out any unnecessary chores or ones you really can do without (see ironing in Chapter Three)
2   Can you afford to get someone else to do some of the chores? For example, a professional cleaner

once a week, a laundromat to fold and dry the laundry weekly, a delivery service for groceries, a part-time or full-time housekeeper to look after the children and do some of the cleaning and/or washing, a lawn mowing and/or gardening service, a bill paying service through a credit card facility now offered by some financial institutions. Tick any chores which you decide to eliminate by handing over to someone else, but do note who will organise and supervise the service.

3 Now write down the tasks left which you enjoy doing. Then get your husband and the children to list what tasks they enjoy doing – or are prepared to do. Work out who is really prepared to take on the tasks and allocate the tasks to the various people – note again who is responsible for what.

4 Now you can all face the tasks left and decide how to manage them. Maybe you can do them on a daily roster. Or put them in a bottle and have a draw each weekend. Or maybe it is agreed to allocate them according to people's expertise.

You might like to simplify tasks by doing things 'in bulk'. For example:
- Shop once a week or once a month.
- Do laundry once a week.
- Pay bills once a month.
- Arrange for a babysitter to come regularly.

Give it a go

Any new system needs a settling-in period. It often helps, too, if people are not only allowed but encouraged to get things done in their own way.

Harry took on responsibility for doing the washing and folding the clothes. He decided to use a local laundromat rather than spend hours at home using the domestic machine. Even though the laundry was not done the same way as his wife would have chosen, everyone was happy with the results.

Raylene and Phil decided to offer their teenage children the 'contract' to clean the house each week. It was clearly worked out for each child which jobs were expected to be done and standards were gradually raised until they were acceptable all round. The children's efforts were assessed each weekend and paid on a 'results basis' to everyone's satisfaction.

Sharing the housework can be fun for young children if we take the time to encourage them and make a bit of a game out of it. They can also learn that they are part of the team and are expected to help run the house.

Unless the responsibility for housework is negotiated fairly in the early days of a marriage it is very difficult to change established patterns later. But it is not impossible. And it is certainly worth striving for a distribution of effort across the family. After all that is part of your taking hold of your life and working towards achieving your next goals!

11 ACHIEVING VISIBILITY

Becoming visible as a person of worth who is capable of making decisions, carrying out tasks and being promoted is still very difficult for a woman in our world today.

Yet we can become less anonymous in order to enjoy some of that success we care about and to have some of our worth as people recognised and utilised. Let us start with a contentious one – how we dress for success.

Dressing for success

By now I hope you have sorted out some of your basic goals and have some vision or dream of how you wish to be living in about five years' time. Maybe you already have a good idea of what you want to be doing in the next decade of your life.

That is great because you can now work back and look at what action you need to take in order to become that kind of person. The first action is to close your eyes and picture how you are dressed in that image of you in the future.

Are you in jeans and a T-shirt hanging out the washing? Are you in paint-smattered clothes finishing off your latest masterpiece? Are you in an elegant suit running that business you have always wanted to start? Are you now boss (and dressed to match) of the organisation in which you are currently working as a secretary? Are you lecturing to or attending influential meetings and looking the part? Have you become so well established that you dress to please yourself and to hell with what others think? Have you at last found the courage to wear the wonderfully imaginative garments you presently hanker after in shop windows?

When to stand out from the crowd
Some of the lessons I have learnt have come from personal experience.

One I remember well from our early days of renovating old houses in an established city suburb. We had been working on the painting and tiling of the house ourselves and had taken a few minutes off to look over a nearby property we were interested in while the agents had it open for public inspection.

I suppose we did look pretty down-at-heel at the time, although we had washed and were not reeking of turps or whatever. I might add that I was fairly well known to several of the local agents at that time. The market was buoyant and many properties were open for inspection twice a week. I often went around to have a look (usually in my more formal clothes) before attending the auctions and several of the agents would often ask my opinion on what I thought the properties were worth, because they knew I was following the market.

The particular agents handling this property were new to the area. They also seemed to have little idea of how fashionable it was for people like ourselves to be doing 'hands-on' renovating. We turned up at the door and were barely allowed in. When I tried to find out what the agent expected the place to sell for he told me condescendingly that he expected it to go for at least $70 000 and was most reluctant to give me the information sheet they had prepared on the building.

I still remember the lesson I learnt that day about clothes and real estate agents. <u>Put on a bit of a show if you want the real estate agents to take you seriously.</u>

On the other hand you might decide not to worry at all about the clothes you have on but casually to drop the information in passing that:
- You already own an investment property in a fast-appreciating area that you might be thinking of selling soon, or
- That you are the investment manager for your company

and may need the agent's professional advice for investing in properties.

Any of these kinds of statements will instantly make you much more visible to the agent who will remember you not as you were dressed but as you might be when you become one of his clients.

On another occasion I planned for the reverse to happen. I had just finished my final exams for my course and was totally numb from the effort of it all. The following day I sat down after breakfast trying to re-order my world and decided I had to do something about my stock of underwear which had suffered from benign neglect for so long that the undergarments I was wearing were in tatters.

Feeling very fragile that day, I decided I could not face any shop assistants treating me with less than the utmost courtesy and dignity. This was particularly relevant as I had to take a robust four-year-old boy and a six months' old baby with me on the shopping expedition.

It was not a day for the old slacks and comfortable, lived-in jumper. I went to my wardrobe and selected a seldom-worn outfit which I believed made me look a very respectable, conservative and reasonably well-to-do matron.

It worked like a dream! I had a very smooth shopping excursion and was accorded just the kind of attention any other well-to-do matron should expect. The shop assistants could not do enough for me and even the children seemed to enter into the spirit of the occasion and acted with much unaccustomed aplomb. I have always remembered how dressing for the situation made it so much easier to achieve the kind of visibility I wanted.

What do both of these stories illustrate? They point to a fact which we often want to ignore or pretend should not be important. Clothes influence enormously how visible we are to people – how well we fit into what they think their kind of clients or employees or associates should look like. When we set up barriers either accidently or

ACHIEVING VISIBILITY

deliberately it becomes much harder for us even to begin to communicate with these people no matter what our skills or abilities are. One phrase I remember sticking in my mind years ago was: 'Dress now to suit the person you want to become.'

I also remember Gwynne's story of how she changed her image and her visibility after a conference she attended gave her some hints.

Gwynne is a solicitor. She dressed pleasantly but was not very differently attired most days from the many clerks and assistants who worked in the legal office. The advice on dress which she heeded and decided to test related particularly to conservative professions such as her own.

It was pointed out to her that since her male associates were used to talking as equals to people in dark suits it would be very appropriate for her to invest in a dark suit also and begin to look more like an associate. She went out and bought a dark suit and a briefcase and was staggered the first day to realise people looked at her from a new perspective.

She had at last become visible to her fellow solicitors as a person like them and they accorded her increased respect and standing from that day on. She also realised she had achieved an important distinction by dressing separately from the office staff rather than merely merging with them.

She bought a wardrobe of dark suits and has never looked back.

I was involved in a research project several years ago where I laid the basis for some long-standing jokes about dress. I cast my eye around the interesting group of women interviewers attired in very varied casual clothing. I then suggested that they would be wise to wear suits or similar outfits in order to appear professional and on an equal basis with the business managers they were to interview.

When some of them questioned this advice I merely pointed out that it would benefit them in their interviews to be visibly more professional than most of the support staff in the managers' offices if they wanted the managers to confide their real opinions.

It worked remarkably well and even though most of the interviewing team were not very familiar with interviewing business people they admitted that they thought the task went smoothly partly because they <u>looked</u> professional.

Looking the part is just as important as being the part!

Dress to suit your industry or environment

Part of becoming more visible involves detective work – observe what other people are wearing, and talk to people you know about what they think is appropriate.

First of all let us be very clear about a couple of things. One is that once you are very successful in your career you are much freer to dress as you want. If you have proved you are the best for the job you are in a strong position by then to dictate the terms, including how you dress, if that is important to you.

The second thing is that once you are your own boss you can also dress to suit yourself. However most of us are in between. If you are in marketing or advertising or design it is highly likely you enjoy indulging your creative urges in your dress as well as in your work. If dressing as an individual is extremely important to you then you need to look for opportunities in those areas where dressing creatively is at least tolerated or is even considered part of the job. Even in the more creative jobs dress expectations can vary from one industry to another as the following story illustrates.

'The wrong woman stood up'

A public relations manager was interviewing applicants for a media representative's position in his department. He noticed two women in his waiting room and knew one of them was an applicant for the position. His first glance told him which one <u>had</u> to be seeking the media position. It was undoubtedly the woman in the smart navy suit, ivory blouse, trim hair style with an attaché case.

However when he asked for Mrs Smith the wrong woman stood up – the woman wearing high-heeled sandals, huge fashion earrings, obvious make-up and a light mauve dress suitable for a cocktail party. She had impeccable qualifications for the position but she had already lost the job because she was 'the wrong woman'.

Mrs Smith had been used to dressing to suit her last position in a high fashion design house. However her current style of dress did not suit this new position in a bank. She was doubly wrong for the job, firstly because she was inappropriately dressed for this particular position and secondly because she had not done the detective work for her new job.

This is an example of how you need to consider how to be visible in the right way.

Choose sensible shoes

One of the important lessons to learn about dress is to adjust to suit your environment. This means wearing flat-heeled, sensible shoes in dangerous situations such as factories or mines or when you are likely to be walking long distances.

I was surprised recently during an informal chat at a committee meeting when one of the men asked me why women wear high-heeled shoes. I had to admit I did not have a good answer. He obviously did not like high-heels and did not think much of the decision to wear them. While he may be in the minority, there is food for thought in his comment. We are more likely to be considered as sensible, responsible decision-makers if we do not trip around in dangerous or frivolous high-heeled shoes.

Smart casual versus smart formal

Many situations in Australia today seem suited to what is termed a 'smart casual' style of dress. This is particularly noticeable in many government offices and in various educational institutions. However if you decide that you would like to aim for a managerial position I suggest you have a good look at what the managers of those offices and institutions are wearing.

If the managers are more formally dressed then you have an excellent clue as to what your new wardrobe might include if you are going to stand out and be noticed as managerial material.

Dressing to suit the job or dressing to suit your ambitions is important but it is also important for you to respect your individuality. If you decide you need to wear suits or formal outfits buy clothes in which you feel good. Enjoy dressing up an outfit with your favourite jewellery, a special blouse you love or a scarf you treasure.

It is just as important to feel right as it is to look right for the situation. And wearing clothes you feel good in can often enable you to appear confident and successful to yourself and to those around you.

Prepare ahead for an interview

Another way you can become visible as the right person for the position is by presenting appropriate written material about yourself. Most positions require some kind of written description of who you are, what your background is and why you should be employed. The usual term for this is a curriculum vitae (CV for short) or a job resumé.

The purpose of sending any information about yourself to a prospective employer (or to an organisation you may wish to join) is to convince those people that you are the right person for the position. It is vitally important that you spend time carefully preparing a job resumé or CV.

I suggest to people that they begin by preparing a very full CV (a mini-autobiography) in order to really sell their skills to themselves. This can then be the basis for a shorter CV tailored to suit a particular position or organisation.

Preparing a mini-autobiography

This mini-autobiography should include the following information:
- your education
- your skills
- your membership of organisations
- your interests and hobbies
- your previous jobs.

Later we discuss how to present this material appropriately for particular jobs.

Education

This should include your high school subjects, the name of your school, the year and level in which you finished school and your results for that year. Next give information about any courses, degrees or diplomas which you have studied since school. List the name of the college, university or organisation which ran the course, the subjects you studied, your results, the type of degree, diploma or certificate awarded and the year in which you finished the course. If your pass levels were not high, it is often best to simply state that you achieved the particular diploma or degree then list the subjects. Finally list any achievements which you remember from your educational years including positions of responsibility.

Your skills

It is best to use verbs to describe your achievements and to use them 'actively' rather than in the passive. There is a certain sense of achievement and dynamism when you say 'planned the 1986 Convention for X' rather than 'helped plan the 1986 Convention for X'.

Here are some verbs to get you thinking about what your skills are: designed, trained, advised, organised, sold, negotiated, invented, initiated, planned, supervised, conducted, created, expanded, counselled, analysed, promoted, expanded, interviewed, wrote, improved.

ACHIEVING VISIBILITY

EXERCISE
Writing it down

Circle the verbs in the aforementioned list which apply to you and then insert them in sentences (see the table). This exercise should help you to phrase some of your skills in sentences with support phrases which show results or evidence of your skills.

Columns I	II III (verb)	IV (object of verb)	V adverb to describe how you did it	VI with the following results.
In order to ………	I			
Examples				
In order to train staff in career development	I designed and conducted	a two day course	effectively	so that I was asked to run three more courses for the firm.
In order to raise money for a film	I organised and negotiated	a government grant	with persistence	so that the film was funded completely for its entire budget of $200 000.
In order to buy office equipment	I researched and analysed	all suitable micro-computers	extensively	so that on my recommendations the manager bought five machines which have been successfully used in the organisation.

Membership of organisations
Here you list all the organisations to which you have ever belonged in the past or at present. These will include political, cultural, feminist, professional, social, fitness, community or interest groups. Note the involvement you had, any positions you held and any achievements for which you worked and which could be the basis of skills you can cite in your CV.

Your interests and hobbies
Broaden your thinking and include here any personal interests you have ever had or pursued. Often these give you clues to job areas you might enjoy exploring.

If you participate in sports, list what level you have reached and the number of years of involvement. Expand on your hobbies, eg any exhibitions you have entered for art, photography or embroidery. List any visits, shows, displays, events, tours or leisure activities that you have organised. Do not stint on your expertise or competence in a sport, a craft or in designing or organising activities.

Your previous jobs
Here you should include all your jobs, paid and unpaid, full-time and temporary.

Start with this year and work backwards through the years, listing the information about each job under the following headings. Go back at least 10 years.

Year Organisation Job title Salary Contributions
                                       to the employer
                                       or organisation

If you have been a full-time housewife for all of those 10 years, write in any relevant position you have held or voluntary work you have done. The following may be a guide:

| 1984 | Home manager Self-employed | Managed the ordering and purchasing of supplies, maintenance of equipment, catering, financial management and co-ordination of team of four in our home. |
| 1985 | Part-time lecturer Self-employed | Sold work on commission, eg crafts. Sub-contracted typing services. |

Homing in on a specific opportunity

Now that you have had practice at writing up your skills, let us consider the situation where you have heard that an organisation is trying to fill a position which might suit you or you have seen a job advertisement for which you would like to apply. This may include a community position on a council or board or even an application for a popular course of study.

If you have not applied for jobs recently do remember that applying for a job and being interviewed are skills which improve with practice. Realise that you will probably need to go through a few interviews before you are offered a job. However, if you sell your skills well you may be just the person they need. And even if you do not get the job, the experience gained will help you with the next one.

Do your homework

Before you compile your specialised CV you should find out all the information you can about the organisation and the job. This will then guide you when you write your CV. These are the kinds of details you should find out:

- who are they?
- what do they do?
- what is their size?
- are they government, semi-government or private?
- what is their address?
- what kind of employers are they?

You can ring up and ask for details about the organisation. Ask for brochures or annual reports or background material on the firm. Explain that you would appreciate the information because you are interested in a job they are currently advertising. One of the best ways to find out more about an organisation is to find people who work there or who are past employees. Try to find friends or acquaintances who could help you here.

A very effective way to find suitable people to talk to is to belong to a network of women who can often locate several of their members for you to talk to in confidence about working for the particular organisation. In Chapter 13, I discuss networking and how to use it.

Here are some questions you would want answered before the interview:
- title of the job
- description of its duties
- job location
- salary/wages, conditions, superannuation, holidays, overtime rates
- work hours and any expected overtime
- age range
- previous experience and/or qualifications required
- person to contact and telephone number or address for further information
- signs of negotiable areas, eg 'salary negotiable', 'flexible hours', 'experience essential/desirable/an advantage' and so on.

The best way to find out more about the job is to ring the contact person from the advertisement or the personnel officer (in a large firm) and ask them what you want to know. Also enquire if they have had or expect many applications for the job and when applications close. Request that a job description be sent to you if one is available. If you are likely to put in your application late, ring up and specifically ask if it will still be accepted. People will often extend deadlines if they know you have requested it for good reasons. Remember to keep a list of queries to ask the interviewer.

The booklet *Going Back to Work* by Iola Matthews suggests the following sources for information on award wages and holiday leave:
- the relevant trade union headquarter if the job comes under a trade union
- the relevant professional association if it is a professional job
- the State Government Department of Labour if the job comes under a State award
- The Conciliation and Arbitration Commission if the job comes under a Federal award.[1]

You might need to check if the job comes under two different awards after you have the job. Try to negotiate so that you are under the best award for you and the one which will keep you on a par with other employees in the organisation.

Writing your CV

Having researched as much information as you can about the organisation and the job itself, you now need to write a concise, relevant CV. For a job early in your career two pages is a good length. If you have had a number of relevant jobs, your CV may extend to four pages. If the position is a senior one expand on your experience, skills and achievements.

Preferably your CV should be typed. Send the original or a very good photocopy to the employer. Keep at least one copy for your records and to take to the interview as a reference. If you have access to a word processor it is much easier to keep a CV updated on a file. Then you can print off new versions as required rather than having to continually retype it.

The following information is required at the top:
- Name
- Address
- Telephone number
- Birth date and other personal details (optional)
- Title of the job and any other details from the advertisement
- Qualifications and education (a summary starting from the most recent and working backwards). Once you have more recent evidence of attending courses it may not be necessary to give your school results. Point out special skills or distinctions or very relevant subjects.
- List your skills and what you have achieved in areas relevant to this particular job. Include voluntary work as well as paid work and link in specific skills to the job description.
- List your jobs starting with your current one and working backwards. Summarise your position and achievements. Highlight the most relevant ones and play down the less relevant.
- Finally include your hobbies or interests if they are relevant to the job, eg photography for advertising, or if they fit in with the organisation or its manager's interests, eg being treasurer of a voluntary organisation gives excellent evidence of budgeting and presenting accounts.

Skills

If the job description asks for a person with initiative to handle maintenance calls your skills might read:
- Experience for three years in taking calls and organising staff to answer queries in the sales department. I succeeded in setting up the referral system to enable staff to return customer's calls within 48 hours. Or
- Experience in calling for contracts and assessing these contracts for maintenance of school equipment as a

member of the maintenance sub-committee of the Burlap School Council.

If the job description asks for a person to organise public relations and run occasional functions for a firm your skills might read:
- Excellent public speaking experience through belonging to a public speaking group for two years. I also participated in a two-day public speaking course at the YWCA in 1983. Or
- Recent speaking engagements have included opening the local school fête as president of the Mothers' Club and leading discussions at group meetings of the Guild. Strong background in negotiating with and liaising press and television when secretary of the Extension Club for two years. Or
- Excellent experience in arranging for both privately catered and outside catered parties of between 10 and 50 people as secretary of the local community club for the past five years. All of these functions have received wide publicity in the media.

Presentation of your CV

Having worked out what to present in your CV you might now like to consider how visible you want to be in the presentation of it. If you are applying for a creative job, a marketing job or one with an unusual organisation which would appreciate signs of talent and initiative, why not use your CV to make them want to interview you.

You could:
- Print it on coloured paper (preferably not lolly pink!)
- Highlight the setting out of the CV with distinctive print or colour underlines
- Design a folder to send it in
- Print it as a scroll and send it in a rolled cardboard container
- Make it the most attractively set-out document you have ever read

- Design a couple of distinctive symbols to divide the CV into sections.

On the other hand, if your potential employer is a conservative organisation, consider how to present a very efficient, well set-out document which is easy to read and looks attractive when you open it. If you are seeking a senior position I suggest putting your CV in a folder because it will stand out from stapled sheets of paper.

A letter of introduction
Always send a letter of introduction with a CV. This letter should state clearly why you are interested in the job and why you believe you are an appropriate person to fill the position.

It should give the job reference number and might also state when you would be available to commence work should you get the job. Keep a copy of the letter for yourself.

Referees
You should seek out and list the names of three referees who could be contacted and who will be relevant to the jobs you are seeking. Always phone and check that the people are prepared to act as referees before you give their names to potential employers.

The interview
This is often the most difficult part. It takes a great deal of practice to be confident at an interview. So it is wise to regard your first few interviews simply as learning experiences.

People often want to talk about how you have tackled particular problems or areas in previous jobs or how you will approach the job you are now being interviewed for. It is important that you answer these questions specifically and do not talk descriptively about your experiences or your ideas if you are expected to give action plans or methods of handling a situation. Many women find it easier to say 'I think' or 'I believe' when they should say 'I set up' or 'I organised'. Practising this can be very useful before you go for an interview.

One of the most effective ways of learning to handle interviews is to have a sympathetic, insightful person give you a tough interview and then review it with you. Tape the interview or put it on video if possible. This can be invaluable in pin-pointing 'waffly' answers to specific questions. Certainly you should think out possible questions and practise how you will answer them.

Some organisations ask questions such as 'What books have you read lately?'. It is worthwhile being prepared with a couple of relevant titles if that kind of question is mentioned by former employees of the organisation as a possible one to expect.

It is also very worthwhile to have a couple of your own questions to ask the panel or the interviewer. This shows you have done your homework and have initiative and have thought about the position and the organisation. Do not be afraid to ask questions about the organisation. You cannot be expected to know all about it before you start working there.

Finally, check when you can expect to be notified about whether you got the job or not. If you do not get the job, ring up and enquire why you did not, as the information might help you in your next job application and interview.

Other ways and means of becoming visible
Tell people you want the position

Whether you are currently employed or seeking a job or a position there are tactics you can work on to become more visible in areas where you need to be viewed as interested and competent.

One of the simplest things is to tell appropriate people what your plans are and get them working for you. If you have your eye on a promotion then you should discuss your ambitions with someone in your organisation who can assist you with advice and can be aware of you as a candidate when the job becomes available. Similarly

ACHIEVING VISIBILITY

if you are looking for a job tell people what kind of job you want. Then they can refer any opportunities to you when they become available.

And if you are interested in becoming a member of a school council or being elected to a local shire or a political position then you need to talk to people about how and when to make an application, organise your supporters and rally your resources. Arrange for supporters to go along and vote for you if you have been nominated to the school council and are facing an election.

In the same way, if you have applied to be considered as a council member of an educational body in response to an advertisement in the press, you need to do your homework and get the support of people who know you, to speak in favour of your being nominated. This is another example of how useful a network can be.

Volunteer to go on committees

Other ways of becoming more visible are often underutilised by women. These include:
- volunteering to do research projects or special reports at work or on a committee
- offering to sit on special committees
- joining professional groups and nominating for a committee position
- volunteering to go on sub-committees if you are a member of a council or big committee
- accepting the position of chairperson when it is offered to you
- offering to go on the finance sub-committee or personnel sub-committee to gain extra experience beyond your current expertise
- using opportunities to go to courses or conferences which could benefit you and the firm
- accepting training opportunities when they are advertised in your organisation
- seeking leadership roles in community organisations to enable you to gain managerial experience

- looking for any positions which can give you a chance to learn new skills.

Further visibility tips
- When you go to a committee meeting be prepared to speak up on a topic about which you are knowledgeable.
- If you are presenting an idea to your organisation make sure you get the credit for it, that you are well prepared and that you can back-up your suggestion with facts and evidence.
- Seek out people you want to keep as future contacts at conferences and meetings. Introduce yourself and ask whether you can have a chat sometime or whether they will send you a paper or publication or whatever.
- Use this method to build up your informal network.
- Use business cards. If your organisation does not supply them get your own personal cards printed with your occupation listed below your name, your home address and phone number and your business phone number if that is appropriate. These are very useful to exchange with people you meet and to give them a means of remembering you.

EXERCISE
Your visibility
Write down any activity you have undertaken recently which has increased your visibility in the marketplace. This list might help you:
- talked to someone about the kind of job or position I would like to have
- started preparing a CV or resumé
- enquired about an organisation I am very interested in joining
- enrolled in a short course to increase any skills or knowledge in my field
- volunteered to go on a committee
- offered to work on a special project

- asked to be sent to a conference
- offered to present a paper on a subject I am interested in to a group of colleagues or an organisation or a conference
- remembered to take my business cards along to a function and gave them to people I met
- introduced myself to a person I would like to know better and got his/her name and address for further contact

Now write down any extra steps you need to take to expand on those you have already taken. Or if you cannot think of any steps you have taken recently to become more visible write down an action plan with the proposed date beside it. Check in a month that you have taken that first step towards visibility.

When you take control of your life and start targeting your dreams, opportunities open up all around you. Do not be afraid of stepping into the limelight.

One of the fastest ways to grow is to take on more responsibility. Then you grow into the role and learn from doing. And those responsible roles are there waiting for you once you seek them.

12 ORGANISING YOURSELF

If you are already employed and have a secretary or a clerk assisting you or if you are a very well organised person anyway, you can skip this chapter, for it deals with <u>very basic</u> ideas and suggestions. However, if you <u>are</u> self-employed or creative or untidy or work at home or you are just starting out in this game of taking hold of your life and trying to become visible, you may find what I have to say brings some order into the potential chaos of your life.

These are the kinds of questions we will address:
- How can we easily find notes on things for meetings and assignments?
- How can we remember things we have to do?
- How can we remember people we have met?
- How can we be more effective in the time we have available?
- How can we ever read all the background material given for meetings or assignments?

Finding yourself some space

Let us start with a very basic suggestion – that by now you need, ideally, a room to yourself in which to study and/or work. However, probably you will not have that luxury. Mine became our daughter's bedroom when she arrived. So we need to look at the next best alternative – a nook of the house or garage or outside retreat – where you can have a desk or table, a chair and preferably some kind of shelves or bookcases, drawers, and even a filing cabinet. Maybe you can make these, or pick them up cheaply or rearrange other furniture to free your favoured item for your own use.

My ideal office would have high open shelves which can accommodate box files and special papers which I like to have handy, a stack of wire boxes on wheels as a handy filing system for current assignments, a huge pin-up board or special board which papers adhere to easily and several deep drawers to keep the things which I think will be useful one day or which I find it difficult to throw away. It would also have a very big wastepaper bin, similar to the cane bin I currently use, to throw out irrelevant mail and other rubbish as soon as it is opened.

EXERCISE
What are your resources?
At this stage you should review your current situation. What space or furniture do you have right now? Do you need more? Write down:
- what items you need
- how you can get them
- who you might need to discuss it with
- when you can mobilise your space and resources.

How to keep track of your notes
The best organised people use folders and binders for notes, which are very useful. There are different types of folders and binders, from simple manila ones to more expensive and sophisticated plastic box/wallet folders.

It would be worthwhile browsing in a good business stationers' shop to view just what is available before you stock up with folders and expensive big plastic binders. There are also many different colours if you want to colour-code different subjects or groups of papers.

Keeping track of lecture notes
I found the simplest system was to have a big punched pad in a lecture binder which I took to all seminars or lectures. I could then keep all my subject folders at home

and would transfer the notes from the main lecture binder to the separate subject folder when I had time to, later.

This saved me having to find different binders for different lectures as I was always in a hurry to get to evening lectures after looking after a baby and a small child.

For my interviews or major assignments I found using a big book very useful. This kept everything together and the book was distinctive enough for me to find easily.

One of the most important lessons I have learnt is to keep things in the same place. I try to discipline myself to do this with keys, books, important papers, notes, files and so on. This is one of the hardest things for a tidy person to understand – that an untidy person can be reasonably well organised because she puts things in a certain place even if it looks a mess. And if people clean up the mess they undo the system.

A simple word about the size of paper

Most businesses use A-4 sized paper for stationery and publications. This is the commonest size of paper. You should consider getting the same sized paper and folders to save yourself becoming mixed up, no matter what size you eventually choose to use.

Have a look at any information sheets or letters you receive. If they are less than foolscap but more than quarto size they are certainly A-4 in size. Again talk to people in a stationery shop about sizes, look at what they have, then decide which size will suit you best.

Keeping track of meeting notes

I am involved with a number of regular meetings for committees, organisations, work assignments and projects and I have finally worked out a system that suits me. I now have a number of box files on an open shelf beside my desk. Each box contains the notes, agendas, minutes and other relevant papers for a particular organisation or committee or project. I also keep a box file for current work enquiries and for information I collect for reference.

How to use box files

These wonderful inventions are like stand-up, sawn-off cardboard boxes. They are available from business stationers and have to be folded and put together. They also need to be well labelled.

I keep the information for the last couple of months for each group, committee or project in its own box. I make sure I always put the notes straight into the box after coming in from a meeting instead of letting them get lost on my desk.

The beauty of using the boxes is that you do not have to go to a drawer to open it or unclip a binder – you simply put the papers into the open box.

When I open the mail I automatically put new information or minutes or agendas for each organisation, committee or project in the front of each box. Then I can easily get the information out, read it and then put it into a folder or wallet or briefcase to take to the next meeting.

Of course you can do the same thing using hanging files in a filing cabinet or using folders or wallets, provided you remember to put all the papers in the right file, folder or wallet after you use them or read them.

For carrying papers around I find the cardboard wallets very useful as papers do not slip out of them easily.

Aids for remembering things

Over the years I have become very reliant on lists. Being the kind of person I am I have found that books get lost less often than pieces of paper. So I keep a big, distinctive book in which to make my lists.

Originally I used wire-bound books for both 'To Do' or 'Action' lists and for recording information when people rang up or for making notes when I talked to people about new projects, and so on. I found this very useful but quite often I tore out a page to give to someone or to take with me if the page had the address on it. That page would inevitably be the one I needed when I was following up details later. I have kept these books dated as I find them useful even several years later for checking up on a preliminary discussion with someone.

Now I use a big diary for my 'To Do' book and for details about phone calls and enquiries. The diary has a day for each page which gives me plenty of space to write my 'To Do' lists each day and to take notes for things I need to follow up later. Quite often this information includes telephone numbers and addresses.

Having the diary as a 'To Do' book means that I can go back to the day or month to find the information I need. It is an invaluable record of my week to week activities. I do not use it for engagements or meetings. It is my personal way of recording and remembering what I have done and what I need to do. My lists combine a variety of tasks from shopping needs, arranging babysitting, calling maintenance people, to returning phone calls, breaking down tasks for big projects and reading briefing notes. Because I have chosen to have an office at home I see my 'To Do' lists as a merging of all of my roles.

The important things with lists are:
- to try to 'prioritise' (which means you mark 'U' for urgent) the urgent tasks, the ones you must do today.
- to cross out or mark the tasks you complete
- to note the tasks you still have to do in the next day's list so you do not forget to do them.

Please note that I use a separate small pocket diary to record all my engagements, meetings and so on. That is my 'real' diary which lives in my desk drawer (in the same place all the time so I can find it) or in my bag or briefcase if I am out.

Aids for remembering people

Setting up a file for address cards and for business cards is an excellent way of keeping track of people's names, addresses, telephone numbers and other details. I have a box of address cards on my desk very handy to the phone.

If possible I try to take down names, addresses and phone numbers straight onto cards when I first talk to a person. Similarly I note down addresses and details of appointments or invitations straight into my diary to save having to do it twice.

The kinds of details you might note on your address cards include:
- the name of the person who referred someone to you or who was the contact
- any special details about the person's position, job, interests
- any personal details, eg children, their ages, serious illnesses, names of husbands or wives, and so on.

I also use my pinboard for lists of addresses of people in groups I belong to for quick reference.

Using time more effectively

Most time-management courses start with people working out their goals. I hope by now that you have done this for yourself at least once.

Others stress using 'To Do' lists, working out which tasks need to be done urgently or are important to do and doing them, and putting any non-urgent tasks in a drawer where you can forget about them.

The main trouble with all of us is that we tend to do the much easier, simple, non-urgent, unimportant things on our list first, and not leave time to do the really important ones which should have top priority.

Breaking down those top priority tasks into step-by-step manageable actions is the best way to tackle them. Spend 10 minutes roughing out a plan of action the first day. Then you can ring people to make appointments, arrange meetings, ask for information, allocate two days of uninterrupted time at home to write the report or whatever. The important thing is you have broken down the difficult tasks into manageable items.

Following up your CV work

As part of organising yourself it is worthwhile writing half a page saying who you are, what you are and a bit about your background. When you are happy with this, memorise it so that when you are asked unexpectedly at parties what you do you will answer with confidence. The half-page summary may also be useful to give to an organisation, firm or potential employer should they require it.

Organising your reading

If you are studying or you find you have a lot of research material or 'heavy' documents to read, you may want to improve your reading skills.

Different situations will require varied approaches to reading. If you know your reading is very slow, consider enrolling for a speed-reading course. However, remember that often technical matter or densely written material still requires slow concentrated reading and thinking in order to understand and absorb it.

Speed-reading can help you skim for the meaning of an article or a book and give you the gist of what it is all about. Then you can decide whether you need to read sections of it in more detail.

Scanning the material first, especially if it is unfamiliar to you, is another method for retaining more easily what you read. Read the table of contents, the chapter headings and any available summaries or reviews of a book. For an article, read the sub-headings and the captions under the photographs first. Previewing the material will help to anchor it in your mind.

Good learners often find these techniques useful:
- read the material aloud and listen to each word you say. Making tapes of key ideas and replaying them in the car or while doing mundane chores can be useful.
- automatically re-read the material until you understand it

ORGANISING YOURSELF

- become 'actively involved' with new information which you think about, challenge and eventually make your own
- analyse material into meaningful categories or sections which can also assist you to learn it more easily.

What is the purpose of this material?

A suggestion for tackling boring books or reports is to work out what you want to learn from the material and how you will benefit from it. Once you can answer this you can either throw the material away as irrelevant or settle down to overcome your initial resistance.

If you merely need to know that the reports have been made and what the main recommendations are, then you can compromise by reading the report summary and skimming any sections of particular interest. If you are expected to give your opinions on a particular part of the report or elaborate on it or assess it then you must read and study it in more detail.

Often when you become involved in meetings, the planning and background documents may overwhelm you. Use some of the reading suggestions here to organise yourself:

- get an overview of important issues in the organisation
- then review where the documents fit into your overall picture
- study the important documents well enough to make a comment especially if that is your field of expertise or interest or representation
- do not expect to understand all the areas at once
- be prepared to ask questions, and to listen and learn from other people's comments about areas you do not understand.

Finally, in any meeting observe the processes that are going on. These are equally as important as the background documents. You can learn a great deal about how the system works by watching the body language, listening to what is being said, noticing who is saying something and who is remaining silent, observing voting patterns and how people support each other.

Once you begin to be aware of these processes you will be better prepared to look at the picture as a whole and to approach your reading load accordingly. The reports will then mean much more to you because of their actual importance or their place in the system.

Also, in meetings listen to what you are intuitively thinking and feeling – heed your overall reactions. Think about <u>your</u> view of things as well as all your observations. And trust your initial view of what is happening. As part of managing yourself respect your intuitive reactions. These can add extra dimensions to your analysis of the reading and your observations of the group.

EXERCISE
Organising yourself
Write down action points to improve your self-organisation in at least one area you need to change. This list might help you, but feel free to add your own points.
- Improve my reading skills.
- Get a big wastepaper bin for my junk mail and rubbish.
- Install a pinboard for address lists.
- Set up a card system for names and addresses.
- Make space beside my phone for a message book and/or a 'To Do' book and/or a box of address cards.
- Get a book to write my action lists in.
- Write down things I need to do in a book.
- Check for any action points I have not done and include them in my new list.
- Sort out and state the actions I must do and do them.
- Sort out and start on my really important action points.
- Set up easy files for my various interests.

- Keep track of my files by putting them in the same place permanently.
- Do a brief CV summary for myself.

Now set a time line for achieving your action points. Check in a month that you have followed up on the actions.

13 WOMEN'S GROUPS: THE NEW STYLE ENTREPRENEURS

In this chapter I want to explore some of the issues involved when we, as women, work <u>together</u> to support each other to achieve our goals.

Some of my feelings of success have come from what I have been able to do on my own, but other very warm feelings of success have come from my experiences of working together with women.

Women's network groups exist in a variety of organisations, although some may not claim networking as their prime objective. Like any group of people, they supply the raw material of the networking concept – contacts who have experience and knowledge we can tap into and share.

Why join a women's group?

Some women do not need to join special women's groups. They have reached positions in their careers or built their own businesses or led satisfied lives on their own and they are happy to have succeeded in the way they have.

Other women find that they have much to share and to gain by joining a women's group. The group may be an informal gathering of colleagues, a small group of professionals, a formal organisation within a company or government department, a community-based self-help group or an official network. The main reason why you might join a women's group is to meet other women in similar situations to your own.

You will, with luck, make new friends and find people who can assist you with suggestions, referrals, even professional advice. You should feel free to use those people, including members you might not have personally met, to assist you in job-hunting and providing useful background knowledge about your industry or your interests.

Depending on what you want from the group and what the group's objectives are you might also:

- enjoy the chance to enrol in courses organised or publicised by the group
- find the opportunity to have your ideas heard and discussed
- have regular social functions organised for you to attend
- gain experience by participating in running activities or team projects
- work to achieve tangible results such as setting up a business or an information centre or an education centre for women
- work towards longer-term social change to enable women to be more strongly represented in politics, in positions of influence and more broadly in sections of the workforce
- work towards specific social objectives such as nuclear disarmament.

Confidentiality

Women can often form friendships, care about each other and draw out of each other information and confidences to an extent which many men are not able to. This ability can be both a strength and a weakness. Sometimes we forget that we need to be wary about disclosing our confidences to other women unless we are sure they respect those confidences.

At other times we need to be constantly vigilant, making sure that we do not accidentally reveal confidential information about our friends, our clients or our organisations to other women simply because they are friends or part of our network.

Two very good rules
- If you do not want anyone to hear about a particular item of information, do not tell it to anyone else at all.
- If you need to discuss a subject with a trusted friend make it very clear at the outset that the matter is totally confidential.

If you have a touchy problem to discuss or an original idea to try out in a networking group, always restate your assumption that the group will respect your confidence.

Here are two examples illustrating the effect confidentiality, or the lack of it, can have on relationships and careers.

Ann had been suggested as a possible member of a board of a public company. She had an excellent professional background and could have contributed a great deal to that company at a board level.

Before the board made the decision to appoint her they made some enquiries of their own. To their dismay they found that she had a reputation for talking to colleagues and associates about lessons she had learnt from various companies in which she had worked. As a result they concluded that she could not be trusted to respect the confidentiality of their board discussions and company policies. In their eyes she was not eligible to be offered a position on the board.

Obviously somewhere in her past she had accidentally spoken out of place to an individual or group. This in turn was interpreted as breaking confidentiality about a client firm. Unfortunately she was never told why her possible board position had not come to pass. She neither had a chance to defend herself nor the opportunity to learn from the experience.

Deirdre ran a successful professional services business. A colleague sometimes referred work to her and was wondering whether to work jointly on projects with Deirdre. But unfortunately Deirdre showed she did not respect the confidentiality of her clients or of her friends on several occasions.

On the first occasion she discussed details of a report she had written. She was also highly critical of the client firm's manager. In this case the colleague, unbeknown to Deirdre, was familiar with the firm and was appalled that she should discuss openly what should have been confidential business.

On a second occasion Deirdre chatted over a networking group dinner with her colleague about mutual business acquaintances. She mentioned details of the acquaintances' financial arrangements which they had discussed with her as a confidant. Again her colleague was horrified that she could not keep her acquaintances' confidences.

This merely confirmed that Deirdre could not be trusted. The colleague no longer refers clients to Deirdre and knows that she could not use her as part of a team.

New ways of empowerment

Networking takes place formally and informally through a huge range of women's groups across Australia. Because of the diversity of the groups from self-help organisations to co-operatives, from political groups to government, educational and individual professional groups there is no single pattern that covers how they all operate.

Perhaps one of the most interesting and encouraging patterns to emerge is that a number of these groups of women have tried to adopt a non-traditional mode of operation. By capitalising on their strengths as women in their new structures they have often tried to avoid hierarchical models and favoured interactive, participative management models.

A number of factors determine how successfully these models work. One of them is the size of the group. According to Mary-Scot Welch some very successful small groups in the United States deliberately have no leaders.[1] Groups which believe that an organised structure is death to women's networking often make a point of guarding against natural leaders assuming power, no matter how helpful they might be. They insist that everyone take a turn irrespective of their leadership ability. Sometimes there is a rotating chairperson whose duty is simply to keep the meeting on the track. A very positive side of this policy is that each member of the group is given the opportunity to learn chairing skills.

The American experience also shows that many leaderless groups are inefficient, unable to reach conclusions or make decisions. Often the first step away from being completely leaderless is to have a steering committee of perhaps six to eight women who make decisions either by consensus or by taking responsibility individually for specific areas. Under this system even if steering committee members recruit support committees from the general members there is no president, vice-president or board of directors and no voting for the general members.

A need for a formal structure

Once any group grows large or intends to grow large it usually needs a formal structure. Depending on the aims and objectives of the group, it may become an incorporated association, a registered co-operative or a company limited by guarantee.

Under a formal structure members are more likely to accept the relatively impersonal power of people who are elected to positions on the committee or board of directors than the personal power of someone who emerges as a leader without being voted in or appointed by group consensus as the official leader.

No matter what the structure is, the group can still be empowered if it uses a participative model to enable the group as a whole to develop its competence, reach its goals and grow in strength and knowledge along the way.

In some situations women have developed and applied sophisticated techniques in using participative models to make their groups work effectively.

I have been employed for two years as a consultant to

Micro Energy, a women's group which has already been effective in achieving its initial goals of developing a business plan and obtaining government support. It now hopes to achieve its longer-term goals of training women in computer skills and running a viable business in training and microcomputer applications.

Here are some of the reasons which I believe contributed to Micro Energy's effectiveness as a group. You may like to check them against your own group's qualities if it is not working as effectively as you had all hoped.

- All of the group's members were both task-oriented and process-oriented.
- The group had very clear goals both in its philosophy and its output.
- The group had a co-ordinator, working group and an advisory committee in its initial stages.
- The group was small (between 12 and 16 people).
- The group was comprised of women with a wide range of skills, all of which were useful to and respected by the group.
- The group drew on the resources of other networks when required.
- The group was in agreement on the actions it wished to achieve and on its broad values.
- The group used a consensus model to reach agreement on basic decisions where there was a potential disagreement on values.
- The group was very aware of the problems for new members of joining a well-established group so they took care initiating new members.
- The group was able to let go of its original goals when they were no longer relevant and adopt new ones.

Behaviour patterns based on sex

Until now the traditional behaviour of men and women in single sex groups has presented different models which are summarised as follows:

Men's only groups
- more highly motivated by problem-solving than women's groups
- impersonal
- competitive
- active participants dominate group all the time and attend meetings very regularly
- less active participants attend less or drop out early
- remarks are made to the group as a whole and tend to be impersonal
- topics chosen are task-oriented
- recognition is accorded to achievements
- mateship is achieved through discussion of events (especially sports) and joke telling
- members repress feelings, show strengths and hide weaknesses
- emphasis on competition, winning and gaining power.

Women's only groups
- less motivated by problem-solving than men's groups
- focus on personal themes and self-development
- collaborative
- wide variation in the level of participation and attendance of participants from one meeting to another
- remarks are made directly to individuals most of the time and are often personal
- topics chosen are process-related
- recognition is based on relationships between people
- closeness is achieved through discussions about personal and family experiences
- members show feelings, hide strengths and reveal weaknesses
- emphasis on self-revelation, drawing out other members of the group and enjoying the experience.

While these models are not true of all men's groups or all women's groups they indicate significant differences in expectations. An interesting comparison to both these models is a summary of some of the behaviour patterns of participants in mixed groups.

Men and women in mixed groups

- produce superior problem-solving
- men talk twice as much as women do
- average men not dominant in men's groups initiate more actions in a mixed group than they would in a men's group
- men's contributions are more highly regarded by both sexes
- women, even those dominant in women's groups, defer leadership and final decisions to men
- lower status is accorded to women by both sexes.

This suggests that both women and men need to learn and to recognise different skills in order to effectively work together and achieve recognition in mixed groups. Some of these skills relate to the concept of 'androgyny' which I will look at in the next chapter.

In the future I believe that, to be effective, many groups including women's groups need to concentrate on developing, within formal structures, their interactive processes. This will give them the benefit of an official leader who is democratically elected combined with the individual strengths of the participants.

Of course the appropriate structure and procedures of any group depend on a number of factors. One factor is how long the group intends to stay in existence. To be effective even a group which meets for an hour needs to have some established procedures to enable it to work, even if it is simply 'socialising'. If a group is to be permanent it needs to have a well defined structure and processes which meet its needs. Another important factor is the type of people involved in the group. There is no doubt that a very valuable person to have in the team is an entrepreneur, preferably a new style entrepreneur who can utilise the group's skills.

What is an entrepreneur?

An entrepreneur is an innovative person who has the drive, the vision and the energy to build a business, a group, an organisation or a project where there was nothing before.

In Chapter Seven I talked at length about 'social entrepreneurs' and the fact that some women workers, both paid and unpaid, direct their drive and energy towards setting up and developing new organisations to meet perceived needs in their community.

In the past entrepreneurs have been regarded somewhat suspiciously by other members of the community. But it is now well recognised that we need to develop and encourage entrepreneurial people to produce and make happen necessary innovations so that our society can cope with changing circumstances.

I believe that women's organisations possess some of the models for developing new style entrepreneurs who will lead us in building the innovative businesses and organisations of tomorrow.

EXERCISE
Do I have entrepreneurial potential?
Think about your answers to the following questions which are based on a host of studies of traditional 'loner' entrepreneurs. Then read about the differences between traditional 'loner' entrepreneurs and 'new style' entrepreneurs.
(a) Do you often sense business opportunities in the areas you have worked in or gained a lot of experience in? (Yes/No)
(b) Do you view your work experience as more important than your past-school education? (Yes/No)
(c) Did you participate in extra-curricular activities such as music, drama, athletics and girl guides while at school? (Yes/No)

(d) Are you a 'job-hopper' (ie often changing jobs)? (Yes/No)
(e) Do you find it difficult to fit into organisational structures? (Yes/No)
(f) Do you have conflicts with authority? (Yes/No)
(g) Do you need to be part of the group and to fit into society? (Yes/No)
(h) Are you a person who has innovative ideas and is able to inspire others to work on them with you? (Yes/No)
(i) Are you prepared to take some personal risks in order to develop an idea you really care about? (Yes/No)
(j) Would you like to be your own boss? (Yes/No)
(k) Do you dislike repetitive, routine work? (Yes/No)
(l) Do you have a high need to be understood, supported and encouraged by others? (Yes/No)
(m) Do you like to retain the control and direction of a business or organisation or idea which you have started and developed? (Yes/No)
(n) Are you a superior problem-solver? (Yes/No)
(o) Can you manage to develop both a broad general vision and the details which are necessary to make the vision work? (Yes/No)
(p) Do you consider people's accomplishments are more important than their feelings? (Yes/No)
(q) Was your mother or father self-employed? (Yes/No)
(r) Do you have a business associate as an influential mentor? (Yes/No)

The key questions for any kind of entrepreneur-loner or new style are (a), (e), (g), (h), (i), (n), (o). If you answered 'no' to (g) and 'yes' to (a), (e), (h), (i), (n) and (o), then you are very much the kind of person who could be entrepreneurial material.

If you filled in all the answers as follows you fit very closely into the research profiles of traditional

> loner entrepreneurs, who were usually men: (a) yes; (b) yes; (c) no; (d) yes; (e) yes; (f) yes; (g) no; (h) yes; (i) yes; (j) yes; (k) yes; (l) no; (m) yes; (n) yes; (o) yes; (p) yes; (q) yes; (r) yes.

The entrepreneurial profile

The entrepreneur is achievement-oriented. He or she wants to accomplish something unique, is prepared to work against a lot of opposition to bring it about and often finds organisational structures restricting. An entrepreneur acts to take personal control of things and plans to make things happen rather than merely waiting to react to crises. Entrepreneurs need good problem-solving skills and mountains of endurance and persistence in order to overcome the many obstacles conservative individuals and organisations put in their way.

Eve Mahlab is an excellent example of a woman who has consistently demonstrated outstanding entrepreneurial drive and flair in both her work in the early days of the Women's Electoral Lobby, a politically active feminist group, and in her highly successful career as a business-woman.

In the early days of the Women's Electoral Lobby she became the group's advocate, its public relations representative, by default. Besides tackling most of the media interviews and public meetings for the group she also put her innovative flair to good use. For instance, she enabled the group to cash in on the results of its excellent survey of the various political parties' candidates' attitudes towards issues of particular interest to women.

It ran a public forum in 1973 entitled 'Why should women vote for you?' as part of the Victorian State election and cajoled the leaders of all the political parties into sharing the same platform to speak to a packed audience of 2500. Her ability to raise funds came to the fore when she negotiated to sell the filming of the forum to television for several thousands of dollars which kept the

Women's Electoral Lobby financially afloat for many years. In response to her desire to work part-time while her children were young, she started her own business. Working from home initially, she developed the basis of her business as an agency that provided employment for women looking for work as legal locums. Drawing on her entrepreneurial sense she developed the consultancy to meet the needs, on one hand, of the many well qualified women lawyers who wanted to spend some time with their young families, and on the other the needs of the firms who became her clients.

Later, when the business was established in more formal premises, she moved into other more predictable spheres of business such as publishing diaries and offering costing services for solicitors. Again she used the untapped resources of skilled women lawyers who wanted to work at home.

Another benefit she provided for her women employees was the finance to allow them to buy property – a rare attitude in a small business anywhere. It illustrates something of the breadth of vision of this woman who saw the opportunity to combine the needs of other educated women with a gap in the market, and developed it into a thriving business while still managing to maintain a good marriage and bring up three children.

New style differences

In contrast to the kind of loner entrepreneur which Eve Mahlab represents, new style younger entrepreneurs who work in teams, rather than as maverick individuals, tend to be better educated than traditional loner entrepreneurs. They are not as impulsive or as concerned about having control and being independent. They are also more adaptive in their approaches to the environment in which they work than loner entrepreneurs.

Women entrepreneurs

Very little research has been done so far on the motives

and profiles of women entrepreneurs. However one preliminary United States study designed to compare female executives with female entrepreneurs looked at 45 executives and 48 entrepreneurs and found that they tended to have more similarities than differences.[2]

The main points to come out of this study were:

- The majority of both groups of female executives and entrepreneurs were either middle or last born, in comparison to conclusions reached earlier that a woman executive tended to be a first and/or only child.[3]
- The dominant motivation for both groups was <u>job satisfaction</u> and <u>professional recognition</u>. Only 13 per cent of the women entrepreneurs stated that the desire to be one's own boss was their principal motivation for going into business. This is in marked contrast to strongly-voiced conclusions from various researchers investigating the motives of traditional entrepreneurs that being one's own boss is a powerful force for men setting up their own independent businesses.
- In keeping with the consistent image of traditional entrepreneurs, this sample of entrepreneurs rated persistence (31 per cent) and hard work (25 per cent) as the main ingredients for their success with only 21 per cent rating 'working with people' as a major component in being successful. In sharp contrast to this, 44 per cent of the sample of executives gave 'working with people' as the essential element for success, followed by 20 per cent who attributed it to hard work. <u>'Working with people' is the difference between traditional 'loner' entrepreneurs and 'new style' team-building entrepreneurs.</u>
- Certainly this sample of women entrepreneurs displayed a less stable job history than the sample of women executives. However other studies show executives can also have many job changes.
- The most common self-concept in occupational roles for both groups was as 'doers'.

In conclusion I believe that we need more women

entrepreneurs in either traditional male roles as lone initiators, planners and builders of new enterprises and organisations, or in new style entrepreneurial roles as inspirers and drivers of groups who can fulfil community and established organisations' needs for new models, innovative projects and novel solutions to today's problems and society's changing values.

Natasha Josefowitz encourages us all when she lists some of those changing values in our society as:
- Placing a greater emphasis on collaboration as opposed to competition.
- Paying attention to process and not just to task.
- Trusting people.
- Sharing power.
- Being authentic as opposed to playing games.
- Appropriately expressing feelings rather than shutting them off.
- Viewing people as whole persons and not just in terms of a job description.
- Accepting and utilizing individual differences instead of resisting or fearing them.
- Showing many personality facets rather than only those related to work.[4]

If she is correct many of us will be at an advantage as we will have already arrived at these values so necessary for the future.

14 WILES AND STYLES: MANAGEMENT, LEADERSHIP AND POWER

What is power?
Power is energy and force. It is what makes things happen. Since decisions are often the first step toward making something happen, power is usually linked with decision-making. So, it follows that if you do not feel free to make decisions about your personal life then you will feel extremely powerless and frustrated.

Once you <u>decide</u> to act in some way to influence where your life is <u>going</u> you are already beginning to tap your personal power reserves which are only as limited as you allow them to be.

What are the different kinds of power?
<u>Roles provide people with power.</u> The roles we often think of when we talk about power are the top positions of an hierarchical pyramid. The people occupying those positions have a great deal of responsibility as well as enormous power in making decisions which affect those below them in the pyramid.

<u>Expertise and skills are power.</u> Highly skilled people have the responsibility and the means to make decisions even in the absence of a defined role. This is particularly evident with scientists and technically adept people. In these cases the authority figure is often the one acknowledged as having the greatest skill or knowledge.

<u>Personal charisma is power.</u> We see this in leaders who

inspire others and are in touch with the ideas and aspirations of those around them in a manner that gives them enormous potential power.

Power often depends on authority. Legal power can give us the authority to act where the law has defined our situation and the decision-making rules which go with it. Alternatively traditions may confer that authority on people. Here power resides in the authority conferred by society, because of commonly-held values and beliefs about behavioural norms, on those who take traditional positions. Traditionally women have had power in the home and men have had power in the workplace.

Personal strength, confidence, assurance and security can give us personal power. This kind of power is what we can all aim to develop for ourselves as the result of our determination to grow and to take control of our lives.

Another type of power, basically negative, comes from some people's needs to be manipulative. These people often take power from others and adopt an arrogant, overbearing, intrusive manner to protect themselves. These are the bullies of the world.

Power can also be derived from reversing people's roles at home and at work, for example when people decide not to perform, or to withhold information or services from those above or below or beside them in the hierachy. It is the power commonly used by workers when they lay down their tools or go slow. The individual can only afford to use this kind of power if he or she is already in some position of power to start with. Of course the effective force of this use of power increases enormously if a big group, like a network or a union, exercises its power. Where it might be easy to replace a single person who refuses to work it becomes much more difficult to replace the whole workforce.

Similarly, combining the power of a number of people or organisations gives the whole group increased power. So groups can also be a source of power particularly for individuals who would not otherwise be able to access power.

How does this affect you?
I believe that you are in a strong position to increase your personal power by improving your skills, gaining more self-assurance, and growing in confidence so that you can make decisions about how to direct your life. Besides concentrating on self-development you could gain more power by establishing your reputation in terms of your skills and expertise in a particular field of interest.

Women also need to gain more impersonal power through taking on recognised roles in our society. We can work to be elected to official positions in government, on councils or committees or be appointed to senior positions within organisations.

Group power which includes the power of refusing to work should also be explored by women if we find that other avenues are too difficult or too slow in opening up opportunities.

Where we realise that people are using their negative power to manipulate us or to deprive us of our rights we would be wise to remember our legal powers. Laws have been passed to try to redistribute power to women and disadvantaged groups. Knowing your rights under these laws is constructive and allows you to use that power.

The power of tradition may be the most pervasive and perhaps the most difficult for any of us alone to do much about. However I believe that significant changes in traditional roles have taken place in the 1970s and 1980s in Australia. As long as enough of us keep challenging the power of tradition, eventually tradition must change.

Other suggestions for personal and group empowerment
One of the ways people in power can deny power to others is to cut off the resources they need to do their jobs. If

you are appointed to a position of power make sure that you have the resources available (money, staff, physical facilities, equipment, rights to use services) to do your job responsibly and effectively.

If you are planning to set up a new direction, start a new business or organise a project, use all your skills to ensure you have the resources you need (with a back-up supplier if necessary) in order to make things happen. Similarly if you are planning, as a group, to work to achieve a goal, work out early how to gain access to the resources you will need in order to reach it. You may be surprised how enterprising you can become in obtaining resources when you know you need them.

Another way people in power can deny power to others is to cut off access to information or distort it. Information is a widely available commodity you can access through libraries, contacts and of course networks. Do not underestimate its importance in your situation.

As an information gathering exercise find out all you can about the Federal Office of Women's Affairs in Canberra and your State government's women's services' office.

You might also enquire about having your name and professional details entered on the State and Federal registers which these offices keep for government boards and organisations to refer to in order to appoint more women to the impersonal power roles in government.

Finally, you can challenge accepted methods of doing things if you are well prepared and have excellent information to prove your point. People often do not expect anyone to challenge them. They may react dogmatically if they have a lot to lose from a change and the least right to maintain the status quo. If you challenge their ideas or their position when you are an expert, or when you are very well prepared and confident with well-researched authoritative information and a well-rehearsed presentation, it will be much more difficult for them to ignore you. And you will have gained considerable power as an individual or as a group in the process.

Leadership
What does leadership mean and how can we develop leadership skills to use in meetings and to manage organisations?

Perhaps you have avoided taking on a leadership role because you have been afraid of being successful, of being the key person, the one with responsibility for running the meeting or the group or the project or the organisation. If you recognise that this has been the case, think again!

You <u>can</u> acquire skills to lead meetings and, eventually groups and organisations, if that is one of your goals. You can also recognise your dominant style of leadership and build up other styles. Just as importantly you can become aware of when to take an appropriate leadership stance. A lot of these skills depend on practice and experience. Start now!

Are leaders born or bred?
Despite much research over the years no-one has come up with a satisfactory answer to this question. There is no doubt that different situations require different styles of leadership. Quite often an emergency may produce a leader in someone who has not displayed signs of having this potential before. On the other hand, people who appear to have necessary potential may prove very inadequate when they assume leadership roles. Either way some leadership skills can be learnt by practice.

A leader is a person who can persuade and direct people to work to achieve goals.

Learning to be a leader
Most groups need leaders. Belonging to a group can offer you a marvellous opportunity to develop your skills

through starting to lead meetings or group discussions.

In any group your formal role will be either as a leader or a participant. As a group leader you are in charge. You can choose to fill the role by setting the agenda yourself or to take a facilitative role by helping others to set the agenda. If you are the chairperson you play a specific facilitative role.

If you are the formal leader of a well-established group you should read the constitution and be familiar with the rules for running the meetings, especially with regard to numbers for a quorum, procedures for special motions and the like. This sort of information is more important than you might think. It may well be that someone else in the group is very familiar with the constitution and can use it at some stage to your disadvantage. It is also important to be familiar with the formal rules for passing motions and so on at meetings. Learning these procedures can increase your confidence and will be invaluable in many other situations later on.

Another worthwhile pursuit is working out what your meetings or discussions need to achieve. This will then help you to determine how you need to run them. Here are some examples of different types of meetings set up to achieve different ends:

A collegiate meeting

This is usually held between people of similar status and/or professional knowledge and skill. This kind of meeting may be appropriate where a problem needs to be solved. The participants need to be given a clear brief of what the problem is if they are to work effectively on solutions. Ideally each person at such a meeting will contribute some knowledge or skill to solving the problem and implementing the solution and will be respected for his or her contribution. Decisions at this kind of meeting are usually made by consensus with the collegiate group being accountable.

A committee meeting

This is one in which representatives from various groups or elected representatives of a larger group meet to make decisions affecting the groups. The committee is the traditional democratic approach to decision-making. Traditionally it has used a voting method for making decisions with the majority winning the issue. In the event of a tie, the chairman usually decides the issue with a casting vote. Accountability for decisions lies with the group, so this kind of meeting requires the attendance of its decision-making participants in order to be effective.

In many situations, committee meetings work better if formal motions are voted on for only key issues. However when policy issues are being debated and decided on you will need to record accurate and formal minutes.

When policy is not an issue but actions are, it is more useful to record action lists with the projected completion date and name of the person responsible for following up the action as the main part of the minutes.

For an effective meeting whether it be for problem-solving or to develop action plans, I have found that using more participative processes involving a scribe and a facilitator enables the group to explore actions, alternatives or 'brainstorm'.

To use this method the group must appoint a neutral facilitator who helps the group focus on its tasks, suggests methods and procedures, enables all members to participate without being attacked for their contributions and keeps the discussion on course. The group also appoints a scribe whose role is to record accurately what all the views and ideas are in the group.

Since in most meetings the chairperson assumes a facilitator's role this method can enable the chairperson to become an active participant along with the other group members. In a business meeting the chairperson may also be the manager who is responsible for all the decisions. If so, this method of running meetings is very appropriate for making consultative decisions or for reaching a consensus. The group or the chairperson may choose to rotate the roles of facilitator and scribe, thus providing excellent learning opportunities for the members in either neutral role.

Adopting this method enables the group to use the resources of its members more fully and explore possibilities before making a decision. This can also 'free' the chairperson to contribute to the discussion, which is often difficult to do when occupying the chair seat.

A negotiation meeting
This is similar to a committee meeting except that decisions are made more on a 'quid pro quo' basis, rather than by voting. Although each group represented may have different objectives the aim of such a meeting is to make decisions on how the various groups can work together to further mutual interests. Each group may seek to achieve the best terms but decisions must be joint ones and all groups are expected to implement the decisions in order to fulfil their own interests.

Advisory meetings
These are usually called to exchange information rather than make decisions. They are concerned with the sharing of facts and opinions and may be called to update people on current issues, to inform them about plans or to give them the chance to contribute information which might then form the basis for decisions at another meeting.

At a more formal level advisory meetings may take the form of interviews (for selection for a position) or consultative discussion.

Command meetings
Here the leader runs an authoritarian-type meeting to instruct or direct his or her followers to undertake or establish rules related to the organisation. The leader decides who will attend the meeting, what the agenda and the objectives are and how the work will be achieved. The

leader, being the only decision-maker, is accountable for all the decisions.

This kind of meeting is not encountered as often as it used to be, perhaps because now many organisations pay at least lip service to democratic values. It is also the least effective method of obtaining employees' support and respect in implementing decisions.

Learning to be an effective leader

Leaders are effective when they inspire trust, give a clear sense of direction and a strong sense of team spirit.

It seems to me that women who want to be leaders need, above all else, determination, confidence, energy and support from family, friends and co-workers. You have to be convinced that you are competent and that you want a leadership role badly enough to make the necessary adjustments in your life.

Once you decide that you do want to learn to be an effective leader here are some of the steps you can take to achieve that.

- <u>Be well prepared for daily events</u> by organising ahead for meetings, keeping informed about inside and outside organisational matters and understanding the current issues. Appear competent and confident.
- <u>Be ready for the unknown</u> by keeping cool and feeling confident deep inside that you can cope with whatever comes along.
- <u>Accept responsibility for yourself and others.</u> Build up an image for reliability and trust with your staff and colleagues. Seek opportunities both for your own growth and that of your staff. Delegate to others the jobs you do well and learn to do new ones yourself.
- <u>Show that you care about people:</u> your manager, your colleagues, your support staff. Be accessible, recognise people's efforts and show genuine concern for people. You do not have to personally help them all but you should be aware when they need help and assist whenever appropriate.

- Develop your creativity in the workplace. This will mean taking risks, initiating projects or changes, forecasting results and financial outcomes, being innovative, solving problems and relating all of these efforts to meeting the goals of your organisation.

EXERCISE
What is your dominant leadership style?
Which of these summaries best describes the way you approach decision-making in a group?

Dictatorial
The leader provides no opportunity for the group to participate. She identifies a problem, considers the possible solutions, makes her decision and then tells the group what they have to implement without considering what they think about the decison.

Persuasive
The leader makes a dictatorial type decision and then persuades the group to accept it. She recognises that there might be resistance to implementing her decision and takes action to try to reduce that resistance.

Consultative
The leader uses the group to explore possible solutions once she has identified the problem. She then makes the final decision herself after consulting with the group and receiving their input.

Participative
The leader identifies the problem clearly for the group and then joins in as an equal to explore possible solutions and decide on the best one. Here the leader not only consults with the group but gives it the right to make the decision itself.

> Note that each of these four styles may be appropriate in specific situations. Now go back to look at the different types of meetings we discussed earlier. How does your main style of leadership fit in with the kinds of meetings you lead at present?

When to consult and when to direct?

Not only will the most appropriate leadership style suit the situation but it should also suit the people you are involved with as a leader.

In a crisis people need to know who is in charge. It may be far more appropriate to issue orders and persuade the group to implement them than to spend precious time and effort on consulting or involving the group in making decisions.

Similarly when tasks are ambiguous, organisational policies are unclear, or members of the group are unable or unwilling, the leader will need to take a direct line on decision-making.

When people in the group are inflexible and relate to rules rather than people's needs they will prefer a directive leader who is non-participative.

Participative leadership works best when members of the group prefer autonomy and self-control. When people can participate in the decision-making on issues which affect them directly, they are committed to the decision and will feel responsible for implementing it.

When is a leader a manager?

A manager is a special kind of leader who has formal authority to work to achieve the goals of the organisation. So a manager needs to combine the qualities of a leader with other practical skills of organising, planning and co-ordinating the staff in order to enable the organisation to do its job.

EXERCISE
Assess aspects of your managerial style
Look at the following list of statements and choose which category (Always, Often, Sometimes, Never) best describes your actions. As a comparison you might like to ask some of your staff to consider how they see you. Then review and possibly discuss the results.

If you are part of a board or a committee which employs people, you also act in a managerial role and might like to consider your board or committee's style of interaction with staff. Often staff of community organisations or voluntary groups suffer because the committee as a whole gives them very little feedback on their performances.

Once you have finished the exercise consider whether you would like to change some of your methods of working to achieve a more effective working environment with your staff.

Aspects of my managerial style
(Your answer should be one of the following: Always, Often, Sometimes, Never.)

I make all my decisions alone.
I consult with others when making decisions.
I do not like to be disturbed.
I am available when anyone needs me.
I keep my door shut.
I keep my door open.
I criticise my staff openly about every error or mistake.
I speak privately to staff about mistakes or frequent errors.
I give praise where it is due.
I seek to offer praise and encourage staff efforts openly.
I do not praise staff openly.
I put my staff's needs first.

I put the organisation's needs first.
I trust my intuitive feelings.
I rely on analysis and advice.
I believe employees' private lives are their own business.
I am interested when my staff talk to me about what they do out of hours.
I keep well informed about the private lives of my employees.
I allow my staff a lot of freedom to use their initiative.
I supervise my staff's work very closely.
I let my staff sort out their own conflicts.
I involve myself in any conflicts my staff have among themselves.
I pass on responsibilities to others whenever I can.
I like to do everything myself.
I keep a lot of information in my head.
I document everything with several backup copies.
I encourage my employees to put forward their suggestions.
I act on suggestions from my employees.

Are women managers different from men managers?

So far there is not a lot of evidence to compare women managers with their male counterparts, mainly because there are still only a small proportion of managers who are women.

Most of the information about managers is male-dominated. For example, when Richard E Boyatzis and McBer and Company developed a model which identified sets of skills that are critical for a manager to possess in order to manage any organisation effectively they based the research on 2000 male managers.[1]

Natasha Josefowitz refers to a study of 36 professional women which found that the majority of that group were overtly humanistic and directed to the 'wholeness' of the human experience.[2] They intensely disliked 'bureaucratic games', meaningless meetings and paperwork. Their commitment was to improve the work environment for themselves and others.

In an article entitled 'A Comparison of Male and Female Business Managers', James D Boulgarides concluded that his study of 108 male and 108 female business managers in the Los Angeles area showed no significant difference between the two groups when they were measured for values and decision styles. The only significant difference was that the male managers earned 14 per cent more than the female managers.[3]

Similarly when comparing values and decision styles for women managers with those of male managers James Boulgarides together with Alan J Rowe and Warren Bennis found that there was no real difference in cognitive styles between men and women in the same field.[4]

However, testing decision styles suggested that successful women executives often possess a unique combination of high conceptual skills and the ability to achieve results in a positive manner by asserting their directive styles. The authors of the article suggest obliquely that women's dominant decision styles may be well suited to the needs of the future manager.

Weston Agore reached a similar conclusion in his United States study of the intuitive decision-making skills of 2000 managers. In all management levels women consistently scored higher than men. Also, women more than men, appeared to exercise a management style which resembled that displayed by top managers. Agore suggests that his criterion may be used in the future to identify women who have the potential for top management positions.[5]

The androgynous manager

Alice Sargent has explored in her book, *The Androgynous Manager*, models of effective managers that are needed for the 1980s. She develops the concept of the effective manager needing to combine the best of traditional male and female traits.[6]

Sargent urges both men and women to adopt different skills to make them better able to cope with the management challenges of the 1980s. Her advice to women is that they should work on directing the implementation of tasks more forcefully; combine expressing their feelings with appropriate use of logic and analysis; promote themselves within their organisations by becoming more visible, by being innovative and by taking risks in initiating projects; make their opinions known clearly and stick by them. Women managers need to become more 'task oriented' as well as 'people oriented'.

Following on from Sargent's notion, here are some suggestions based on the ideas in Chapters 13 and 14 which may help you to be more androgynous when you work in mixed groups and meetings:

- Aim to talk to the whole group as well as to individuals. Use eye contact to include the members of the group when you address them.
- Show your strengths to start with and only reveal weaknesses or personal details about yourself once you know the group will respect you for that.
- Be ready to accept any suggestions of chairing a meeting or taking a position on the committee when it is offered to you.
- Be clear which positions you wish to fill on a committee. If you are interested and could learn from the experience offer to be treasurer or vice-president or president. Alternatively, being membership officer or the person responsible for organising the group's activities can open up the network potential of the group to you. Use the opportunity to make yourself and your talents known to members at functions.
- Use the formal moving and seconding of motions and records of minutes of meetings to assert yourself.
- Move or second several motions in a formal meeting

and check that your name has been recorded by the secretary in the minutes.
- Read the minutes before the meeting and raise the matter beforehand or at the next meeting if you find that some points have not been recorded accurately.
- Check that your own ideas or statements or contributions have been correctly noted in the minutes. If necessary draw attention to the fact that they have been omitted altogether, incorrectly quoted or attributed to another person.
- Offer to set up and chair a sub-committee or special group to explore an issue in which you are interested or already have expertise or experience.
- Speak up on any issue you are interested in and aim to build up your reputation for expertise in that area over a number of meetings. If necessary, frequently repeat your ideas or refer to your expertise (table something you have published or drop a reference to a conference you attended on the subject) in meetings until people in the group view you as the group authority in that area.
- Compete for something you want and negotiate with individuals to gain their support if appropriate.
- Where possible back up your case for a new idea with expert opinions and research before you have to defend it.
- Give support to those whose views have merit even if few in the group favour them.
- Co-operate with others when you agree with their proposals.
- Share your ideas, dreams and experiences with people who respect you. Be prepared to listen to theirs as well.
- Be prepared to defend an issue and show anger or sorrow or any other emotion if in your opinion it is an appropriate response.
- Confront those you respect on issues you disagree with and do not allow it to affect your relationship afterwards.

- Push for the implementation of your initiatives.
- Claim ownership of initiatives or reports which you have been responsible for or which have passed on up the line in your organisation.
- Be prepared to back down graciously and admit you were wrong or that the issue is over before you become obnoxious.
- Take risks. Analysing mistakes provides an excellent basis for learning on the job.
- Trust your instincts about people you meet.
- Use empathy and intuition to supplement your logical analysis of a situation when making decisions.
- Be sensitive to the people involved in any proposals or decisions and draw on your common sense when judging how it will affect them. Be prepared to suggest they be actively involved in the decisions if these will impinge seriously on their lives.

Working to adopt and assimilate the best of both male and female traditional strengths will eventually make you feel more of a whole person, able to choose from various sides of your personality at will and to enjoy being both tough and tender, confrontational and cooperative when appropriate. You will find it very empowering to eventually be able to work at ease in both mixed and single sex groups gaining from the advantages of both and cross-fertilising ideas from one group to the other.

You will also have learnt to cope with some of the challenges of the future where adaptability, skills in interpersonal relationships, empathy and innovation will all be needed.

EXERCISE
A personal review
Think carefully about this chapter. Then write down the most important message, if any, that will assist you in achieving your goals. Think why the ideas meant something to you. Write down your thoughts.

What action might these suggest you take?

If this involves changes in the way you act at present how do you think it will affect your colleagues, family, friends and support staff? How will you deal with those reactions?

Write down your proposed action and a realistic date for you to review your progress.

15 THE OLDER AND WISER YOU: PAMPERING YOURSELF

In this chapter I look at what you might do to take control of your life and enjoy it more as you get older! It assumes that you have come to one or more of these conclusions:
- you do deserve to look after your own self more at this stage of your life
- you are leading a successful life but it is palling a bit at the moment
- you would like to feel a bit more excitement in your life with or without a partner
- you need to taste life more fully
- you can afford to leave your family and dependents to look after themselves occasionally while you have some time to yourself
- your life is becoming more hectic and you want to be able to enjoy it more
- you want to broaden your horizons before they narrow forever.

EXERCISE
Review basic self-care
How long is it since you had any of these?
- a thorough medical check-up
- a dental check-up
- a new hairstyle
- a facial
- a manicure
- a spa bath

THE OLDER AND WISER YOU

- a sauna
- a massage
- a splurge on clothes

Maybe the first step you should take is to check on your personal health before your life grows busier.

The joys of relaxing your body

There are various books available on the techniques of massage. There are also regular courses run by adult education organisations which can teach you these techniques and enable you to practise under supervision.

Learning to massage each other may be a skill you and your partner could acquire to add another dimension to your life together.

If you have never had a spa, a sauna or a massage give it a go. One way to find out if you enjoy it is to visit a health centre, either public or private, and find out what they have to offer.

Another way to treat yourself to some of these experiences is to book yourself in for a few days or a week or longer at one of the residential health care centres especially established to relax you and put your life back on an even keel.

EXERCISE
Review your health care
Write down what exercise you have had over the past two weeks. Here are some suggestions to jolt your memory:
- walking
- climbing stairs
- tennis (or other organised game)
- gym
- running
- jogging
- swimming

> - private exercises at home
> - bicycling
> - going to an exercise class
> - doing jazz ballet
> - doing yoga.
>
> Depending on how you responded, write down what action you are going to take to make sure you stay fit and healthy.

Taking time off by yourself

I believe that you need some time by yourself to unwind, especially if you look after young children. Even if you are only able to take off a few days you will come back refreshed and able to see your children with new eyes.

As you grow older and you become involved with managing your own interests as well as catering for the needs of others, you will need to ensure that you make space to take time off. The best way to do this is to plan ahead. Put it in your diary. Make the arrangements you need well ahead of time and let everybody know that you will not be available during those dates. If it is likely to be a problem do not tell people where you are going. Certainly do not tell them if you are intending to stay at home.

Taking time off may simply mean taking a week or a fortnight of your holidays and 'doing nothing' at home. If you work hard outside the home you may find that having time at home to potter around and catch up on what is happening with your friends and neighbours is the most relaxing thing you can do.

Alternatively taking time off may mean you need to get away from everyone for a while to have a different kind of holiday. Or you might like to do some of the things you really enjoy such as skiing or sailing or simply driving in the car like a gypsy till you find somewhere interesting to stay.

To do this you may need to come to terms with the idea of going on a holiday alone or with a friend, if you have always relied on your family for company. Increasingly I meet women who discuss how they go on holidays separately from their husbands to enable both of them to enjoy separate interests.

Corinna realised early in her marraige that her husband was not interested in travelling. So she often went on very memorable trips with her sister or their sprightly mother, leaving the men at home to enjoy their own company.

On the other hand Martina and her husband both enjoyed travelling but found it difficult to take time off together and leave their young children. They also realised that Martina preferred a holiday which gave her the opportunity to do a number of different things while her husband preferred to simply lie on the beach and unwind for two weeks.

To satisfy them both they decided to take holidays alone at different times each year as well as having a family holiday all together at Christmas. This meant each of them could be responsible for looking after the children while the other was away. It had the added value of giving them each time to develop further their individual relationships with their children.

Where to go?
This is a list to start you thinking about what you can do when you take time off by yourself.
- Enjoy yourself at home.
- Go off to the snow or the beach or the mountains.
- Drive around exploring your own state.
- Go on a boat trip – anywhere.
- Take a skiing holiday in New Zealand or USA or Europe.
- Get fit and go for a hiking trip in Tasmania.
- Get fit and go for a walking tour of Nepal.
- Take a trip to a place you have never visited but always wanted to go to.
- Hire a farm house and commune with nature for a while.

- Take a weekend package trip to Sydney or Hobart or the Gold Coast or Singapore or Hawaii.
- Go camping.

Acquire new interests
Another path you might choose to explore as part of taking time off is developing new interests and skills. Some holiday packages cater especially for people who want to learn new sporting or craft skills. You may choose to spend a sporting holiday at a centre which specialises in teaching people better skills at specific sports like tennis or diving or skiing.

Another idea would be to time your holidays to coincide with a special course you would enjoy doing. This could be for a few days or longer at your local adult education centre.

If you are a collector, you might choose to spend your time avidly searching for new specimens or visiting exhibitions in which you are interested.

Taking time off together
Besides allowing space for yourself to grow and to renew your reserves of energy you may also need to make efforts to allow space for your husband or partner so that you can develop your relationship further.

Bringing up children often crowds out the opportunity for a couple to have time alone together. One of the best plans might be for you both to arrange to take a couple of weeks off together and leave the children with friends or relatives or even a paid housekeeper. But often this is not possible for a variety of reasons, in which case you both have to be more resourceful to ensure you keep your relationship alive and well in the face of possible erosion from constant family intrusion.

Here are some suggestions to start you thinking:
- Shut the door on the rest of the family and take time to talk together undisturbed.
- Go for a swim or a walk or a bike ride together.

- Go for a daily run or jog together in the morning or at night.
- Have lunch together occasionally.
- Have lunch together on a regular day each week or fortnight.
- Go dancing together.
- Do something you have both always wanted to do together.
- Go camping or bushwalking together.
- Join a gym and go together during the week or at weekends.
- Have breakfast together at a restaurant.
- Arrange for a babysitter to come on a particular night each week and go out together that night regardless. Take turns to decide what to do each week even if it is simply talking over a coffee or going for a walk along the beach.
- Book in for a romantic 'night away' in your own town or city. Book into a motel or hotel for dinner and stay the night. Have breakfast in bed the next morning and wander around your town or city as a 'holiday-maker' for the day. You may be surprised how rejuvenating one night away can be for a relationship. And you can usually manage to find someone to look after the children for such a short time.
- Book in to do a course together on some other interest you both share and can enjoy doing together.
- Take a packaged weekend away to another town or state or to Singapore or wherever.

Once you have arranged for time out for yourself and for your partner you are free to explore these other suggestions for surviving with dignity as an older and wiser woman.

Learn to say 'No'!

One of the main lessons we all have to learn as we get older and busier is to say 'no' firmly and graciously and persistently, if necessary. This is not related to suitors or wooers but to the people who so often look to you to give of your time freely to help them or their group with no sign of your being paid in return.

Once you become established you may find that other people expect you to pass on your experience to them for nothing in return. If you are happy to do this then go ahead. But I suggest that somewhere along the way you will have to say 'no' in order to survive. Ask for travelling costs if it is a long way to travel, or tell them you charge an hourly fee for any engagements at all, or ask for a 'trade-off' in return. The 'trade-off' might simply be the right to come back and ask a favour later or to use some of the person's or organisation's contacts or resources.

Using services

One way of making your life a bit easier is to look for people who deliver goods, who call round to your house to perform services and who can do things for you, even at a cost, which can save you time and energy. These are services you might consider looking for:

- a dress shop that will bring a selection of suitable clothes to your home and allow you to choose which ones you like
- a hairdresser who will visit you at home
- a grocer, supermarket or green grocer who will deliver your goods, preferably when you order them by phone
- a speciality cake shop for special occasion cakes
- an excellent delicatessen that can provide you quickly with a variety of goods for entertaining at short notice
- a catering firm that can supply you with a dinner party or a feast and provide the staff as well so you can relax and enjoy your entertaining.

Coping with travel

If, as part of being older and wiser, you will need to travel more – here are some of the things to consider to make yourself more comfortable.

First, be prepared with a small sewing kit, some band-aids and headache tablets for an emergency. These are standard for me in my briefcase these days anyway! Next, if you travel frequently by air, take the initiative and join one of those airlines' organisations (eg Flight Deck, Golden Wing or Captains' Club) which pamper you when you have to wait around a lot at airports. Don't ask your organisation whether you <u>may</u> become a member or not. Simply join up and charge the cost to your organisation or firm. If there is a fuss, pay for it yourself! You will then have somewhere convenient to wait, a place where you can have a shower to refresh yourself, make phone calls, entertain people if necessary. It should make life much more comfortable for you.

I always try to travel light and carry my bag into the cabin with me to save having to wait around for the baggage to come through. This is much more convenient especially if you have a busy schedule or an early appointment.

Consider taking a taxi to and from the airport rather than driving yourself. It will be much more relaxing for you and you can use the time to catch up on reading, or sleeping if necessary. You might also consider hiring a chauffeur-driven car for a day in a strange city if you have a number of widely-spread places to visit and do not want the hassle of trying to find a taxi each time you need to move to a new location. If you intend using taxis try to check on their availability well before you need to leave for your next appointment. On several occasions I have been surprised when it has taken me an hour to find a taxi to come to the factory I was visiting.

Overseas travel
One of the main things to learn to cope with is jet lag. This can affect you not only on the long flights between countries, but also on the shorter internal flights, if you are especially susceptible to the conditions in the cabins of aircraft which may result in swollen feet and feelings

of exhaustion or stomach upsets for several days.

In order to look after yourself you should try to avoid drinking alcohol on flights and eat sparingly. For your swollen feet it is recommended that you rub them with hand cream or a similar type of cream which is soothing to the tingling nerve ends. There are also special creams available at chemists for rubbing into your feet.

Doing exercises while sitting in the plane is another excellent way of keeping the circulation moving in your limbs. This means tensing and relaxing the muscles of your feet, legs and thighs consciously and regularly during the flight. You can also buy special cushions to rest your feet on if you are travelling on long journeys. These help you to exercise the muscles and relieve some of the strain of travel. Of course the more you are able to walk around, especially during stop-overs, the better for you and your circulation.

Apart from the tangible physical symptoms of sore feet, jet lag mainly refers to the upset in our daylight/dark cycles when we travel from east to west or vice versa. The situation is worse when you travel in an easterly direction even if you are returning home.

As long as the time zones remain constant it is not so upsetting for our bodies. However if our biological clock is still operating on local time in a changed time zone we will be at our least effective in making decisions and being alert and confident when we first arrive in a new location. Here are some hints on coping with time-zone changes.[1]

- Re-time your sleep and meals to local times as soon as you arrive in your new location.
- If possible arrive in the evening and get an early night's sleep for the first few nights.
- Allow yourself at least 24 to 48 hours before undertaking strenuous events, though ideally you should allow yourself five to nine days to adjust.
- Have plenty of non-alcoholic drinks to make sure you

THE OLDER AND WISER YOU

do not become dehydrated on the flight.
- Eat sparingly on the plane especially during at-home sleeping times.
- Speed up your rate of recovery by adjusting your hours at home before your flight takes place.
- Do outdoors exercise such as going for a brisk walk to re-orient your body to its new time schedule rather than sitting around having a nap and a read.

Once you arrive at a hotel these hints will assist you, particularly if you are on official business and are travelling alone.
- From travel agents find out which hotels cater for business travellers or ask the hotel itself when making bookings. You are more likely to be treated as a professional in a business-oriented hotel than a tourist hotel.
- Make arrangements well ahead if you require catering and meeting rooms as these are usually handled by separate divisions within the hotel itself.
- Let the hotel know that you are there on business by indicating who made your booking when you ask for your reservation at the desk.
- Ask about any services you may require (eg dry cleaning) when you check in.
- A word to the bartender that you do not want to be disturbed should enable you to have a drink in peace at the end of the day if you are concerned about being viewed as a potential pick-up.
- If you are entertaining people at dinner make it clear that you are paying for the meal when you make the booking.

Staying in a hotel room alone can be a very exhausting experience. So if you are travelling overseas for the first time begin looking for some contacts who can look after you. These may be family friends or relatives if you are fortunate enough to have international connections. Or your own organisation may have arranged some introductions for you with their associates in the country you are visiting. If you are already in a group with international representation it will be easier to arrange these introductions.

Do tell people you are going away and ask for recommendations based on their experience of what to see and what to expect. Often you will find that friends have unexpected contacts in the place you are visiting or have had some interesting adventures themselves in the cities you are bound for. Even if what people say is not very encouraging be ready to form your own conclusions about your destination when you get there. Your own attitude will partly determine how you enjoy any new experience, including this trip. Look forward to it with anticipation.

Have some fun in your life

Finally, let us think about the older and wiser you. Are you enjoying your success? Take time to appreciate what you have done so far with your life. Give yourself a chance to unwind a bit and enjoy life.

How long is it since you did something outrageous? If you do not do it now when will you? Keep sight of your goals. Enjoy your experiences and your achievements now.

16 WHAT IS THE NEXT STAGE FOR YOU AND YOUR DAUGHTERS?

Targeting success for you is a personal adventure – yours alone. You only have to be concerned with what you aim to do to feel successful. Even if what makes you feel successful may leave others entirely unexcited or unsympathetic. You don't have to worry yourself about their opinions. Feeling successful is part of you making sure you get some of the things you want out of life now no matter how old you are.

Success can come from completing tasks and achieving action plans which make you feel good. Targeting success begins to add a zest to living which eventually enables you to take control of your life, seize opportunities and enjoy them.

If you are wondering where to go from here, compare the changes which have occurred especially in the first five years of the 1980s in the opportunities for women in Australia. Although you still have to seize the opportunities yourself, there is more support and acceptance of women doing a variety of things than there was even five years ago.

Let me encourage you with a summary of the women who were featured as the 15 fastest growing company managers in the USA in 1984. According to the list, 13 of the women had children, mostly grown up.

The youngest manager was Sally Field, of biscuit fame, who was only 29. However in the other fast growing companies, the managers were considerably older with two in their thirties, four in the forties, five in their fifties, three in their sixties and one aged 73![1]

Most of the women started their businesses part-time from home but several of them took over and developed family businesses.

You have the chance to develop your opportunities now to be successful in your life no matter how old you are. Why waste the opportunity to be able to do things you always wanted to do now if you are mature and experienced? To extend your planning try thinking about what you can do in the next decades of your life.

EXERCISE
The decades of your life
Take a big sheet of paper and draw seven or eight columns for the decades of your life going up to the eighties and nineties. The first column is for your youth and teens. The other columns are for each decade of your life up till now and into your future. Now label the columns as follows: Teens, Twenties, Thirties, Forties, Fifties, Sixties, Seventies, Eighties, Nineties.

For each column up to this point in your life write down the main things you have done. These might be interests, experiences, sports, hobbies, travel, work, family, study or anything else special for you. Now go on to the columns in your future life. Think ahead to what you see yourself doing at least in your next decade.
- Will there be new and different interests?
- What special experiences are you saving for your next decade?
- What sports will you be playing?
- Would you like to travel? What places would you like to visit?
- What hobbies will you be enjoying?

Success for younger women
So far I have tended to concentrate on finding success once you have a family and are looking to develop other interests. I realise this is of little use to younger women who may be wondering how to find different patterns of combining their established careers with meaningful relationships and/or having children.

In this section I want to explore some of the trends which appear to be encouraging young women to target success through demanding paid careers early in their lives. I will also examine some of the research on how younger, successful, ambitious women view themselves in relation to the idea of combining families and future careers.

Many of today's young women face quite different situations with regard to having families and careers to those of the generations of women before them. This situation exists in the mid 1980s mainly because of the push in the 1970s by older women to enable women in general to become more visible in society, to gain more equality in decision-making and to be able to choose to lead a variety of different lives including the traditional ones of wives and mothers. Now we are beginning to see the fruit of that hard work.

The problems and opportunities of the transition
Of course we still have a long way to go in being able to achieve a balance between the aspirations of both the supporters of equal opportunity legislation and the young and not-so-young women in Australia today and the prevailing attitudes of the environment in which we live.

This in-between stage is a difficult one with, for example, most of our society still geared to children being cared for by mothers in the home or by teachers at school.

Eve Mahlab saw a potential opportunity in the wealth of talented women who were busy looking after their families and built her innovative Australian company using professional mothers' services on a part-time basis. Another firm adapting to the needs of its female staff is Casto Travel, one of the top 60 'fastest-growth companies' in the United States according to *Savvy*. The manager, Maryles Casto, plans to initiate innovative benefits such as on-site day care, optional four-day working week and one-year maternity leave for her employees.

At present in Australia plans to bring in permanent part-time work and job sharing are still embryonic in most private organisations. Few people, whether they be men or women, have work situations in which they are able to combine their jobs with having contact with their children even on the odd occasions when the children are simply not very well.

Perhaps the most difficult thing to acknowledge in our current situation in Australia is that generally it is still very difficult for a woman to successfully combine having a family, a meaningful marriage and satisfying paid work.

Recently I was encouraged by the results of a survey of 200 Sydney-based women in management.[2] Many of the women were finding opportunities to develop their talents in managerial positions particularly in private enterprises. Half of these women were married and 36 per cent of them had children.

However a startling finding was that many of the women felt that their role as home-maker had had a dampening effect on their careers to the extent that almost a third of the women said that on reflection they might have forgone having children in order to be able to better pursue their careers. In addition almost a quarter of the women had made a conscious decision not to have children in order to pursue a career.

The researchers got the impression that the decision not to have children would not be necessary if maternity leave and flexible work conditions were available in the private sector and if women did not have to choose between losing their status and promotional prospects, and taking leave to have a family.

This survey highlights the dilemma many younger women face as they pursue careers and have to decide whether to try to juggle a career and a family. It is a dilemma many women have not had to face in the past. It also underlines the fact that many of the conditions necessary to enable women to take more responsible positions in paid work situations have not been achieved. Obviously other changes in work conditions still need to be developed before these career women can feel free if they want to achieve success as mothers.

What does the future hold?

I believe that this transitional stage we are going through does provide opportunities for those able to seize them.

Some of these opportunities are in setting up businesses that provide services for women who want to pursue raising families with successful careers. Already there is a growth in the number of women running speciality shops providing catering services and gourmet take-away meals.

There may be a market for 'home managers' who offer services and people to run all aspects of a home including paying the bills and managing the maintenance as well as getting supplies in and looking after the children.

Similarly, educational institutions might look at providing courses specifically geared to training people as 'home managers' along the lines of a day course offered in Melbourne in 1985 which likened the skills involved in running a home to those of running a small business.

Other possibilities might result from the opportunities to convert our homes into part-time or full-time 'electronic cottages' using the varied communications devices of the 1980s and 1990s.

In the happiest situations whole families may be able to share work situations with various members of the family working part-time on domestic tasks, part-time on paid work tasks and still having the chance to relax and enjoy other activities.

There is no doubt children will have a different notion of work if they live in this environment. It may also bridge the gap between their lives at school and home and their parents' lives at work.

Certainly there are issues of working at home which need to be addressed such as how to walk out of the office and shut the door, how to cut off your work from the rest of your life and how not to have clients or your boss feeling free to contact you on a seven-day-a-week basis. But combining work and home even on a temporary basis may offer many mothers of the future more opportunities to enjoy varied work than they have at present.

Maybe women will be the ones to initiate imaginative new housing projects or design new settlements which can support child-care and community-care, including services which will make it easier for dual career families to lead busy lives and also look after families and each other. These settlements will need to be along different lines from some of the housing developments in Australia which have tended to offer isolated dwellings in remote, newly developed suburbs. Many of these are planned assuming that the mother will be constantly available to provide taxi and pick-up services for the members of their families when public transport services are inadequate.

These kinds of suggestions may provide the bases for some of the changes which will have to take place to enable us and our daughters to be able to choose to succeed in the future.

That target: success

So after all this what exactly is success for you?
- Is it starting to feel you are in control of your own destiny?
- Is it planning to do something and realising a few months later that you have actually done it – and it worked?
- Is it relaxing and acknowledging that you want to enjoy

looking after your family right now knowing that you can set goals for yourself in years to come?
- Is it realising that you have talents you have not even explored yet – and that now is the best time to start?
- Is it you struggling to overcome the barriers of a lifetime in order to prove to yourself that you can achieve something which is very important just to you?

One of the most rewarding things for me is the feeling I have so often of being in harmony with my world. I treasure the fact that I enjoy so many of the activities which keep me busy. And I am encouraged by the growing number of women who share this sense of joy in a life well and fully lived.

REFERENCES AND FURTHER READING

CHAPTER 2
1 Penelope Russianoff, *Why Do I Think I am Nothing Without a Man*, Bantam Books, New York, 1983.
2 Natasha Josefowitz, *Paths to Power*, Addison-Wesley, Reading, Mass, 1980.

Further reading
Gail Sheehy, *Pathfinders*, Bantam Books, New York, 1982.

CHAPTER 3
1 Betty Friedan, *The Feminine Mystique*, Victor-Gollancz, London, 1963.
2 Colette Dowling, *The Cinderella Complex*, Fontana, London, 1981.
3 Judy Lever with Dr M Brush and Brian Haynes, *PMT The Unrecognised Illness*, Outback Press, Melbourne, 1979.

REFERENCES AND FURTHER READING

Further reading

Hazel Edwards, *Houseworking – the Unsuper Person's Guide to Sharing the Load*, Dove Communications, Blackburn, Vic, 1984.

Dr Irene Kassorla, *Putting It All Together*, Warner Books, New York, 1973.

Maureen Minchin, *Food For Thought*, Alma Publications with George Allen & Unwin, Melbourne, 1982.

Theron Randolph & Ralph W Moss, *An Alternative Approach to Allergies: The New Field of Clinical Ecology Unravels the Environmental Causes of Mental and Physical Ills*, Lippincott & Crowell, New York, 1980.

Gwen Wesson, *Brian's Wife Jenny's Mum*, Dove Communications, Blackburn, Vic, 1975.

CHAPTER 4

1 Jo Kinross & Sylvie Shaw, *Minding Your Own Business*, Cassell, North Ryde, NSW, 1980.

CHAPTER 6

1 Martina S Horner, 'Femininity and Successful Achievement, A Basic Inconsistency' in Michele H Garskoff (ed), *Roles Women Play: Readings Toward Women's Liberation*, Brooks/Cole Publishing, Belmont, California, 1971.

2 Colette Dowling, *The Cinderella Complex*, Fontana, London, 1981.

3 Patricia Grimshaw & Lynne Strahan (ed), *The Half-Open Door*, Hale & Iremonger, Sydney, 1982.

Further reading

Dr Irene Kassorla, *Putting It All Together*, Warner, New York, 1973.

CHAPTER 7

1 The *Australian*, 24 April 1985, p 12.
2 John Larkins & Bruce Howard, *Sheilas: A Tribute to Australian Women*, Rigby, Adelaide, 1976.
3 John Larkins & Bruce Howard, *Sheilas: A Tribute to Australian Women*, Rigby, Adelaide, 1976.
4 John Larkins & Bruce Howard, *Sheilas: A Tribute to Australian Women*, Rigby, Adelaide, 1976.

REFERENCES AND FURTHER READING

5 Antoni Sachi, 'The Script, a Bigger Role for Women' in the *Age*, Saturday Extra, 22 June 1985.

CHAPTER 8
1 Alice G Sargent, *Beyond Sex Roles*, West Publishing House, St Paul, Minn, 1977.
2 Iola Matthews, *Going Back to Work*, Rigby Instant Books, Adelaide, 1977.
3 Stress Scale reproduced with permission of Pergamon Press, New York, and Dr Thomas H Holmes, Professor, School of Medicine, Department of Psychiatry and Behavioural Sciences, University of Washington, Seattle. See Holmes, T H and Rahe, R H: The Social Readjustment Rating Scale, *Journal of Psychosomatic Research 11*:213-218, 1967, for complete wording of the items.
4 H Benson & M Z Klipper, *The Relaxation Response*, Collins Font Paperbacks, Glasgow, 1975.

Further reading

A Kirsta, 'Breathing Your Way to Beauty', in the *Australian*, 8 May 1985, p 11.
G North & H J Freudenberger, *Women's Burn-Out*, Doubleday, Sydney, 1985.

CHAPTER 9
1 Alice G Sargent, *The Androgynous Manager*, AMACOM, New York, 1983.
2 David A Kolb, *Learning Style Inventory*, McBer & Co, Boston, 1976. (Local suppliers are Power Human Development in Sydney and Melbourne.)

Further reading

Jilly Cooper & Tom Hartman, *Violets and Vinegar*, George Allen & Unwin, London, 1980.
Lore Harp & Eliza G C Collins, 'The Entrepreneur Sees Herself as Manager', in *Harvard Business Review*, July-August 1982.
Gwen Wesson, *Brian's Wife Jenny's Mum*, Dove Communications, Blackburn, Vic, 1975.

REFERENCES AND FURTHER READING

CHAPTER 10
1 Judith Ward, 'Back to School after 25 Years', in the *Australian*, 2 October 1985, p 18.
2 Doctoral research conducted by Susan Kelly, lecturer in Psychology at Swinburne Institute of Technology, Melbourne.
3 Bettina Arndt, 'How the Balance of Power is Changing in Marriage' in the *Bulletin*, 16 April 1985, pp 58-65.

Further reading
Jeanne Bodin & Bonnie Mitleman, *Mothers Who Work – Strategies for Coping*, Ballantine Books, New York, 1983.
Hazel Edwards, *Houseworking – the Unsuper Person's Guide to Sharing the Load*, Dove Communications, Blackburn, Vic, 1984.
Francine S Hall & T Douglas, *The Two-Career Couple*, Addison-Wesley, Reading, Mass, 1979.

CHAPTER 11
1 Iola Matthews, *Going Back to Work*, Rigby Instant Books, Adelaide, 1977.

Further reading
Richard Nelson Bolles, *What Colour is Your Parachute?*, Ten Speed Press, Berkeley, California, 1985. This book is updated annually.
The Catalyst Staff, *Marketing Yourself – The Catalyst Women's Guide to Successful Résumés and Interviews*, Bantam Books, New York, 1981.

CHAPTER 13
1 Mary-Scot Welch, *Networking*, Warner Books, New York, 1981.
2 Donald L Sexton & Calven A Kent, 'Female Executives and Entrepreneurs a Preliminary Comparison' presented in *Frontiers of Entrepreneurship Research: Proceedings of the 1981 Conference on Entrepreneurship at Babson College*, edited by Karl H Vesper, University of Washington, Seattle.
3 Margaret Henning & Anne Jardim, *The Managerial Woman*, Pocket Books, New York, 1977.

REFERENCES AND FURTHER READING

4 Natasha Josefowitz, *Paths to Power*, Addison-Wesley, Reading, Mass, 1980.

CHAPTER 14
1 Richard E Boyatizis, *The Competent Manager*, Wiley-Interscience, New York, 1982.
2 Natasha Josefowitz, *Paths to Power*, Addison-Wiley, Reading, Mass, 1980.
3 James D Boulgarides, 'A Comparison of Male and Female Business Managers', in *LODJ*, 5 May 1984, pp 27-31.
4 Alan J Rowe, Warren Bennis and James D Boulgarides, 'Desexing Decision Styles', in *Personnel*, January-February 1984, pp 43-52.
5 Weston H Agore, *Intuitive Management – Integrating Left and Right Brain Management Skills – How to Make the Right Decision at the Right Time*, Prentice-Hall, Englewood Cliffs, New Jersey, 1984.
6 Alice G Sargent, *The Androgynous Manager*, AMACOM, New York, 1983.

Further reading

Rosabeth Moss Kanter, 'Women in Organisations: Sex Roles, Group Dynamics and Change Strategies', in Alice G Sargent (ed), *Beyond Sex Roles*, West Publishing House, St Paul, Minn, 1977.
Rosabeth Moss Kanter, *The Change Masters*, Simon and Schuster, New York, 1983.

CHAPTER 15
1 The *Australian*, 2 May 1985, p 21.

CHAPTER 16
1 Kimberly A Brown & Carol Perkin, 'The Savvy 60', in *Savvy*, April 1985.
2 *Australian Business*, 2 October 1985, pp 94-98.

Further reading

Rada Rouse, 'Working with Great Expectations', in *Portfolio*, August/September 1985, pp 43-44.
Alvin Toffler, *The Third Wave*, Pan Books, London, 1980.

INDEX

achievements, 53-4
action points, 41, 64-71, 107, 113, 134
androgynous manager, 217-20
assertiveness, 145, 151-2
Atkinson, Sallyanne, 89

burnout, 111-12

career paths, zig-zag, 85-9, 93-6
change, 40-4, 101-14, 118-31, 153-9
　feelings and, 21-2, 34-6
　uncomfortable, 21-2, 34-6, 99-102
Child, Joan, 87-8
choices, 6
committees, volunteering for, 119, 177-8
communication, 143-51
competence, interpersonal, 123-5
confidentiality in women's groups, 191-3
conflict, 127-8
confrontation, 127-8
control, 1-3
criticism, coping with, 121
curriculum vitae, 166-70, 172-5, 186

decision making and power, 204
depression, 28-31
　pre-menstrual tension and, 29-30
dreams
　future, 60-3, 118
　past, 3
dress, for success, 160-6

Edwards, Hazel, 49-50
empowerment
　group, 206-8
　personal, 123-5, 193, 206-8
entrepreneurs
　new style, 197-8
　social, 89-92
　traditional, 198-203
　women, 198, 201-3
exercise guidelines, 110-11
exercises
　Assess aspects of your managerial style, 215-16
　Assessing your capacity to grow, 118
　Coping with the rate of change, 113
　Daring to dream, 118
　Decades of your life, 234
　Do I have entrepreneurial potential? 198-200
　Exploring dreams, 4-5
　Feelings of success, 45-7
　Future scenario, 60-3
　Goal review, 134
　Household tasks, 156-9
　How crowded is your life at present? 135-8
　How to use this risk-taking assessment, 18
　Interpersonal competence, 124-5
　Life events as sources of stress, 104-6
　List of opportunities and achievements, 53-4
　Making lists and changing what to do, 8-9
　Organising yourself, 188-9
　Personal review, 220-1
　Review basic self-care, 222-3

INDEX

Review your health care, 223-4
Sources of stress we take for granted, 108-9
Stress events in your recent life, 106-7
What are your dominant values? 57-8
What are your resources? 181
What is your dominant leadership style? 213-14
What were your answers? 83
What you might begin to change, 38-41
Will success change you? 83
Writing it down, 168
Your risk-taking potential (so far), 13-18
Your own zig-zag path, 96
Your visibility, 178-9

fear
　of risk-taking, 10-19, 21-5
　of success, 72-4, 76-83
feelings and change, 21-2, 34-6
Field, Sally, 233
fitness, 36-7
Fitzgerald, Kaaren, 90-1

Gazzard, Marea, 93
goals, setting of, 61-71, 113, 117-19, 120, 134
groups
　effective, 193-5
　men's only, 195-6
　mixed, 197
　participative model in, 194-6
　women's, 190-1, 193-6
grow, capacity to, 118-30

Harp, Lore, 126
health, 109-14, 222-4
　see also stress management

household
　managing of, 40-4, 135, 138-40, 143-59
　problem solving, 153-4
　sharing, 41-4, 143-5, 154-9

interviews, preparation for, 166, 175-6

jet lag, coping with, 229

leadership, 124-5, 208-9, 212-14
learning style, 130-1
letter of introduction, 175
lists, 9, 148-50
Lovell, Pat, 93

Mahlab, Eve, 200-1, 235
managerial styles, 214-16
managers
　androgynous, 217-20
　women, 216-20
Medaris, Helen, 49
meetings
　facilitator's role in, 209-11
　participation in, 209-11
　types of, 209-12
micro-energy, 195
mid-life crises, 55-6, 74-5

networks, 190-4
Nicholson, Joyce, 78
Nursing Mothers' Association of Australia, 91-2

opportunities, 53-4, 71, 82, 170, 233, 235-8

participative model in groups, 194-6
Paton, Mary, 91
Pleasance, Barbara, 50-1
politics, careers in, 87-9
potential, developing, 27-8, 60-71

INDEX

power
  decision making and, 204
  roles and, 204
  sources of, 204-6
pre-menstrual tension and depression, 29-30
problem solving in the household, 153-4

referees, 175
relationships, 6
relaxation response, 109
rest, 103
resumé, preparation of, 166-70, 172-5, 186
risk-taking, 10-19, 21-5
  fear of, 19-20
  self-confidence and, 22-3
  survival and, 23-5
  taboos and, 19-20, 25-6
roles and power, 204

Schoenbaum, Golda, 50
self-confidence, 22, 31-3
  and risk-taking, 22-3
self-esteem, 22-3, 31-3
self-image, 122
self-talk, 31-3
social entrepreneurs, 89-92
society, value changes in, 203
stress management, 103-13
study
  effect on marriage, 142-3
  further, 131-4, 138-45
success
  and women executives, 217
  dressing for, 160-6
  family influence on, 51-3

fear of, 72-4, 76-83
feelings of, 21, 45-54, 74-5, 233, 238-9
patterns, 45-51
Sudden Infant Death Research Foundation, 90-1
survival
  and risk-taking, 23-5
  tactics, 7, 10-12

taboos, 25
  and risk-taking, 19-20, 25-6
Thatcher, Margaret, 117
time-management skills, 8, 185
travel, 228-32

Vallentine, Jo, 88-9
value changes in society, 203
values, 55-9, 61-3, 84-5
  conflict in, 56-8
visibility, 126-7, 160-6, 176-9
volunteering for committees, 119, 177-8

Ward, Judith, 141-2
weight, losing, 37-8
women entrepreneurs, 198, 201-3
  household managers, 7
  managers, 216-20
women executives and success, 217
women's groups, 190-1, 193-6
  confidentiality in, 191-3
working at home, 237-8
Wright, Sharon, 50

zig-zag career paths, 85-9, 93-6